CALIFORNIA WILDLIFE VIEWING GUIDE

Jeanne L. Clark

ACKNOWLEDGMENTS

Special thanks for advisory assistance to all of the California Watchable Wildlife Project committee members: Joe Holmberg, U.S. Army Corps of Engineers; Paul Brink and Lillian Andris-Olech, Bureau of Land Management; Will Tully and Len Seifreid, Bureau of Reclamation; Bob Garrison, California Department of Fish and Game; Joe Engbeck, California Department of Parks and Recreation; Ed Kress and Lou Koe, California Department of Transportation; John Poimiroo and Flo Snyder (ret.), California Office of Tourism; Dick Cunningham and Mietek Kolipinski, National Park Service; Charles Houghten and Denise Dachner, U.S. Fish and Wildlife Service; Joelle Buffa, U.S.D.A. Forest Service; and John Schmidt, Wildlife Conservation Board.

Thanks are also due to Oren Pollack, The Nature Conservancy; to Sara Vickerman and Wendy Hudson, Defenders of Wildlife; and to Delo Rio-Price and Charly Price, illustrators. Heartfelt appreciation is extended to the literally hundreds of on-site managers and others who provided nominations, interviews, tours, and text reviews.

Finally, a special thank-you is extended to Caltrans for providing all of the binocular and directional signs on interstate and state highways, and to the many county and city public works departments statewide that have also joined as partners in signing the viewing network.

Author and State Project Manager:
Jeanne L. Clark

National Watchable Wildlife Program Coordinator:
Kate Davies, Defenders of Wildlife

Illustrators:
Del Rio-Price and Charly Price

Front Cover Photo: Sea Otter, Monterey Bay   JEFF FOOTT
Back Cover Photos: Mirror Lake, Yosemite National Park   LEONARD PENHALE
Cinnamon Black Bear, California Sierras   ART WOLF

CONTENTS

PROJECT SPONSORS

 DEFENDERS OF WILDLIFE is a national nonprofit organization of more than 80,000 members and supporters dedicated to preserving the natural abundance and diversity of wildlife and its habitat. A one-year membership is $20 and includes six issues of the bi-monthly magazine, *Defenders*. To join or for further information, write or call Defenders of Wildlife, 1244 Nineteenth St., NW, Washington, DC 20036. (202) 659-9510.

 THE CALIFORNIA DEPARTMENT OF FISH AND GAME owns and manages more than 150 wildlife areas and ecological reserves and twenty-two fish hatcheries, encompassing more than 520,000 acres of unique natural habitats. The Department of Fish and Game's mission is to protect and manage the state's diverse fish, wildlife, and plant resources, and the habitat on which they depend, for their ecological values and for their use and enjoyment by all Californians. You can support wildlife conservation efforts by joining the California Wildlife Campaign or purchasing hunting and fishing licenses and stamps. Department of Fish and Game, 1416 Ninth Street, Sacramento, CA 95814, (916) 653-1856.

 THE CALIFORNIA DEPARTMENT OF PARKS AND RECREATION operates 276 park units that encompass 1.3 million acres and experience eighty million visitor days per year. Acting on behalf of present and future generations of Californians, the Department of Parks and Recreation provides opportunities for healthful outdoor recreation and acquires, protects, develops, and interprets an extraordinary range of irreplaceable natural and cultural resources. You can support the park system by purchasing annual passes or publications. Department of Parks and Recreation/Room 118, 1416 Ninth Street, Sacramento, Ca 95814, (916) 653-4000.

 THE CALIFORNIA DEPARTMENT OF TRANSPORTATION (Caltrans) designs, builds, operates, and maintains the State's transportation system. Caltrans' mission is to provide a safe, efficient, dependable, and environmentally responsible transportation network that moves people, goods services, and information quickly, safely, and efficiently throughout the Golden State. Caltrans is supporting Watchable Wildlife by providing binoculars signs at interstate and highway exits near sites throughout the state. Department of Transportation, 1120 N. Street, Sacramento, CA 95814 (916) 654-4817.

THE BUREAU OF LAND MANAGEMENT cares for 17.2 million acres of land in California and is the nation's largest conservation agency. The Bureau of Land Management manages public land under a multiple-use concept that includes environmental protection, resource development, and recreation, in a combination that will best serve the needs of the American people. Thirty-eight management areas throughout the state offer diverse wildlife viewing experiences. Bureau of Land Management, 2800 Cottage Way, Sacramento, CA 95825 (916) 978-4746.

THE BUREAU OF RECLAMATION manages 1.6 million acres in California which are used to store and supply water for irrigation and for use in homes and factories. The Bureau of Reclamation also generates hydroelectric power, provides flood control, and helps meet fish and wildlife needs, recreation needs, and water quality standards. The Central Valley Project provides irrigation water and urban water; about 200,000 acre-feet of water is provided to wildlife refuges and wildlife areas in the Central Valley. Bureau of Reclamation, 2800 Cottage Way, Sacramento, CA 95825, (916) 978-4919.

 THE NATIONAL FISH AND WILDLIFE FOUNDATION, chartered by Congress to stimulate private giving to conservation, is an independent not-for-profit organization. Using federally funded challenge grants, it forges partnerships between the public and private sectors to conserve the nation's fish, wildlife, and plants. National Fish and Wildlife Foundation, 1120 Connecticut Ave., Washington, DC 20036, (202) 857-0166.

 THE U.S. FISH AND WILDLIFE SERVICE administers 326,992 acres of land and water in California, including thirty-two national wildlife refuges, two wildlife management areas, and one fish hatchery. The mission of the U.S. Fish and Wildlife Service is to conserve, protect, and enhance fish and wildlife and their habitats for the continuing benefit of the American people. Programs include the National Wildlife Refuge System, protection of threatened and endangered species, conservation of migratory birds, fisheries restoration, recreation/education, wildlife research, and law enforcement. Anyone can help acquire and conserve wildlife refuge habitat by purchasing Federal Duck Stamps. U.S. Fish and Wildlife Service, Reg. Director, ARW, 911 NE 11th Avenue, Portland, OR 97232, (503) 231-6214.

 THE U.S.D.A. FOREST SERVICE manages eighteen national forests in California encompassing more than twenty million acres. The U.S.D.A. Forest Service's mission is to manage resources to benefit the public while protecting them for the future. The Eyes on Wildlife program enhances opportunities for all people to experience wildlife, fish, and plant resources and encourages the public to support conservation efforts. You can become a partner in the Eyes on Wildlife program by contacting the nearest national forest. U.S.D.A. Forest Service, 630 Sansome, San Francisco, CA 94111, (415) 705-2874.

 At FORD MOTOR COMPANY, our goal is to incorporate environmental stewardship into all of our actions. By using a fundamental approach called "Quality Environmental Management," all Company components must consider potential environmental impacts in the development of products, processes, and projects. We have a long history of supporting numerous environmental activities and are very proud to be counted among those supporting Defenders of Wildlife.

Other important cooperators include:
U.S. Army Corps of Engineers • California Office of Tourism
National Park Service • The Nature Conservancy
Wildlife Conservation Board

December 23, 1991

In the United States, California's diversity of wildlife species and natural habitat is unparalleled. From rugged coastlines to spectacular mountain ranges, and from the valleys to the deserts, California's more than 100 million acres offer an opportunity to view some of the world's most stunning natural settings.

These lands sustain more than 1,275 species of mammals, birds, reptiles, amphibians, and fish. The range of wildlife is amazing, from monarch butterflies to elephant seals, and from plodding desert tortoises to swift tule elk. Many of these species are protected in sanctuaries set aside especially for their safety and preservation.

Finding, observing, and enjoying the state's wildlife heritage has now been made easier, thanks to the California Wildlife Viewing Guide. Developed cooperatively by more than a dozen agencies and conservation groups, it encompasses federal, state, county, and private viewing areas in every county of the state.

Watch the highways for brown road signs with the white binoculars symbol. They lead to each of the sites described in the guide, and to memorable opportunities to enjoy California's wildlife bounty.

Sincerely,

PETE WILSON

INTRODUCTION

From wave-battered headlands and quiet estuaries to spectacular mountain peaks and sprawling desert plateaus, California's world-famous scenery is a haven for wildlife. The diversity of habitats and wildlife species here are the greatest in the United States.

California's 101 million acres include 1,100 miles of coastline, 37,000 miles of streams, and more than 5,000 lakes. Habitats range from 14,495-foot Mt. Whitney, the tallest peak in the lower forty-eight states, to Death Valley's Badwater, the lowest point in the Western Hemishpere at 282 feet below sea level. The variety of wildlife is stunning, from feather-light monarch butterflies to two-ton northern elephant seals, from slow-moving desert tortoises to peregrine falcons that fly at speeds of 160 miles per hour. California boasts:

- The largest wintering population of bald eagles in the lower forty-eight states.
- The oldest living trees on earth, the 4,600-year-old bristlecone pines, and the world's tallest trees, the redwoods.
- Several places to see a million waterfowl during the peak of migration.
- Clusters of more than 100,000 monarch butterflies on coastal trees.
- The tallest coastal dunes in the western United States, some reaching 500 feet, and home to several vulnerable nesting species.
- Animals such as tule elk and southern sea otters, returned from the brink of extinction due to protection and management.

California also has the largest population of any state and more than 280 rare, threatened, and endangered plant and wildlife species. This crush of people literally has changed the face of the land, placing many species and habitats in jeopardy. Several of the sites in this guide were acquired to protect prime wildlife habitat or vulnerable species. These sites allow viewing without causing harm to either the land or the animals.

Nearly 300 natural areas were considered for the California Wildlife Viewing Guide, and stringent standards were used to evaluate and choose 150 of them. Almost every California county is represented. Many worthy sites were not included due to space and several more were eliminated to protect wildlife and habitat from damage.

Whether your destination is a two-acre tidepool or 600,000 acres of desert park, this book can guide you to many memorable wildlife viewing experiences. May it also inspire you to support agencies and private organizations that are working to safeguard California's wildlife and wildlands legacy.

THE NATIONAL WATCHABLE WILDLIFE PROGRAM

California's wildlife viewing opportunities exist because outstanding natural areas have been purchased and set aside for a variety of recreational uses. For many years, state and federal wildlife land acquisitions were funded almost entirely by sportsmen through license fees and taxes on hunting and fishing equipment. These refuges, wildlife management areas, preserves, preservation programs, and habitat enhancement activities clearly benefit non-game species as well.

Today, hunting opportunities and revenues are decreasing just as threats to wildlife and habitat are becoming more acute. At the same time, wildlife viewing activities have increased significantly.

The California Watchable Wildlife Project is part of a national response to this interest in wildlife viewing and the need to develop new support for wildlife programs. As part of the National Watchable Wildlife Program coordinated by Defenders of Wildlife, fifteen government agencies and private organizations in California joined forces and funds to promote wildlife viewing, conservation, and education. The California Wildlife Viewing Guide is an important first step in this effort.

This book is much more than a guide: the sites are part of a wildlife viewing network. Travel routes to each site will be marked with the brown and white binocular sign appearing on the cover of this book. Travelers may also notice these signs in other states. Eventually, the United States will be linked by a network of wildlife viewing sites, as similar partnerships are formed in other states.

The partnerships formed to produce the California guide and viewing network will continue to work together on site development, interpretation, and conservation education. In addition to such well-established programs as the U.S. Fish and Wildlife Service's Federal Duck Stamps, several new wildlife viewing and conservation programs are evolving, including the Department of Fish and Game's California Wildlands Campaign, the U.S.D.A. Forest Service's Eyes on Wildlife, and the Bureau of Land Management's and U.S. Fish and Wildlife Service's Watchable Wildlife.

Use this guide to plan outings that coincide with peak wildlife viewing periods. Consult it while traveling for interesting side trips. Take advantage of on-site education programs. And support wildlife agency and private efforts to fund and conserve wildlife programs by becoming an active partner in resource stewardship.

Mirror Lake, Yosemite National Park LEONARD PENHALE

BIODIVERSITY IN CALIFORNIA

Biological diversity, or biodiversity, is a term used by wildlife experts and land managers to describe the variety of wildlife and the natural processes that maintain healthy natural communities. A. Starker Leopold once commented that "...the welfare of a Sharp-shinned hawk is inseparable from the welfare of the small vertebrates on which it feeds, and it is impossible to consider the one without the other." Managing for biodiversity involves understanding these relationships and saving the processes that connect wildlife to each other and to their environment.

Water is one of the most important forces shaping California's wildlife habitats and biodiversity. Through a complex process, water moves from the ocean, to clouds, to lakes, wetlands, and aquifers, down rivers, and back again to the ocean. From the abundant lakes and rivers of the Shasta Cascade region to the arid washes and playas of the Southern Desert, the presence or scarcity of water affects California's plant and wildlife communities.

Each chapter of this guide is introduced with an illustrated biodiversity theme. The illustration includes species, habitat, and ecological processes common to sites in that region; water, or the lack of it, plays a prominent role in each theme.

The North Coast theme, for instance, explores the role of wetlands. The Central Valley theme goes one step farther, showing how California wetlands are connected to other countries by well-travelled Pacific Flyway migration routes. The South Coast illustration shows how development has restricted riparian areas, wetlands, and beaches.

The state's diverse habitats and water patterns not only sustain wildlife. Stunning scenery and varied climates have attracted thirty million people, the highest population in any state. Grazing, logging, mining, agriculture, water diversions, and development are just a few activities that support the state's populace. They also eliminate wildlife habitat and can interrupt the processes that tie wildlife and the land.

Today, more than ever, management and conservation of the state's biodiversity require cautious stewardship, widespread public interest, and new sources of support. Visit the sites in this guide and look for the ties between the land and the species it supports. Witness the courtship rituals of sandhill cranes or the noisy battles of elephant seals and feel a connection to these ancient, natural processes. Finally, get involved. Become a partner by pledging time or funds to help assure that the biodiversity for which California is so famous is preserved for the generations to come.

VIEWING HINTS AND RESPONSIBILITIES

- Plan your visit around peak viewing seasons or times of activity. The first and last hours of daylight are often the best time to see or photograph wildlife. Remember, some species are nocturnal.
- Use field guides, checklists, and other resources to identify species and learn about habits and preferred habitats.
- Use binoculars, spotting scopes, and your ears to locate wildlife.
- Move quietly and by yourself, when possible. If in a group, allow for periods

of silence. While viewing, honor the rights of other site visitors.

- Be patient; spend time in the field. Many species have outstanding camouflage or adaptive behaviors that keep them well-hidden. Some may leave when you arrive but may return shortly. Don't expect to see all the species listed in the guide during one visit.
- Watch for wildlife where two habitat types meet. This "edge" offers good viewing because of the many types of food and cover it provides.
- Stay on marked trails and use binoculars or zoom lenses to extend your view. Hide behind vegetation or your car. Be careful not to damage or trample plant life.
- Refrain from touching, feeding, or moving too close to wildlife, their nests, or dens. Leave seemingly abandoned wildlife alone. If you are concerned about an animal, report its location to the site managers.
- Maintain a safe distance from dangerous wildlife, such as rattlesnakes, mountain lions, and black bears. Be aware that these animals could be nearby if you are visiting wildlands habitat.
- Honor the rights of private landowners at or near viewing sites.
- Leave each site undisturbed and respect rules regarding pets, collecting, viewing hours, etc. Pick up litter and dispose of it properly.
- Come prepared. Whether you are going to the ocean, where there may be dangerous surf, or the desert, where conditions can be harsh, plan ahead and bring all of the things you, your group, or your vehicle may require. Remember that many of the sites in this guide are not developed.

HOW TO USE THIS GUIDE

One hundred and fifty sites are grouped in eight regions. Color bars on the edges of the pages help identify each region. Each region begins with an illustrated biodiversity theme on the left page and a map and site list on the facing page.

Each **site name** is preceded by a **site number**. This number appears on regional maps and in the index.

The **description** gives a very brief overview of featured wildlife and habitats. It is followed by viewing information that includes species, reliability of viewing, and best **viewing seasons**. Viewing tips are offered. *NOTES OF CAUTION RELATING TO ROAD CONDITIONS, SAFETY, VIEWING LIMITATIONS, AND OTHER RESTRICTIONS APPEAR IN CAPITAL LETTERS.*

Directions to each site are written. Supplement them with regional and county road maps and watch for the binocular signs. Road signs can be stolen or vandalized—don't count on them to get you to the site.

Ownership refers to the agency or group that owns or manages the site. A **phone number** is listed after the owner to use for more information about the site. If there are several owners, several phone numbers may be listed, following the same order.

The **size** of each site is offered, followed by the **closest town** that offers gas, food, and lodging.

At the top of each description, **wildlife symbols** are used to feature the types of species that are common. Near the end of the description, **recreational icons** provide information about the facilities at each site.

FEATURED WILDLIFE

 Songbirds Perching Birds

 Waterfowl

 Upland Birds

 Wading Birds

 Shorebirds

 Marine Birds

 Birds of Prey

 Hoofed Mammals

 Carnivores Mammals

 Small Mammals

 Reptiles Anphibians

 Freshwater Mammals

 Seals, Sea Lions, Sea Otters

 Whales Dolphins

 Fish

 Tidepools

 Bats

 Insects

 Wildflowers

 Hoofed Mammals

 Small Mammals

FACILITIES AND RECREATION

 Parking

 Entry Fee

 Restrooms

 Handicapped Accessible

 Picnic

 Restaurant

 Lodging

 Camping

Hiking

Cross-country Skiing

Bicycling

Boat Ramp

Large Boats

Small Boats

In this guide, the handicap accessible symbol means there is at least car viewing and one handicapped-accessible restroom on site. Wheelchair-accessible trails are noted when possible. Please call for more detailed information.

SITE OWNER/MANAGER ABBREVIATIONS

ACE	U.S. Army Corps of Engineers
BLM	U.S. Bureau of Land Management
DFG	California Dept. of Fish & Game
DPR	California Dept. of Parks & Recreation
DWR	California Dept. of Water Resources
NPS	National Park Service
USBR	U.S. Bureau of Reclamation
USFS	U.S. Forest Service
USFWS	U.S. Fish & Wildlife Service
TNC	The Nature Conservancy

HIGHWAY SIGNS

As you travel in California, look for these signs on inter-states, highways, and other roads. They identify the route to follow to reach wildlife viewing sites.

CALIFORNIA
Wildlife Viewing Areas

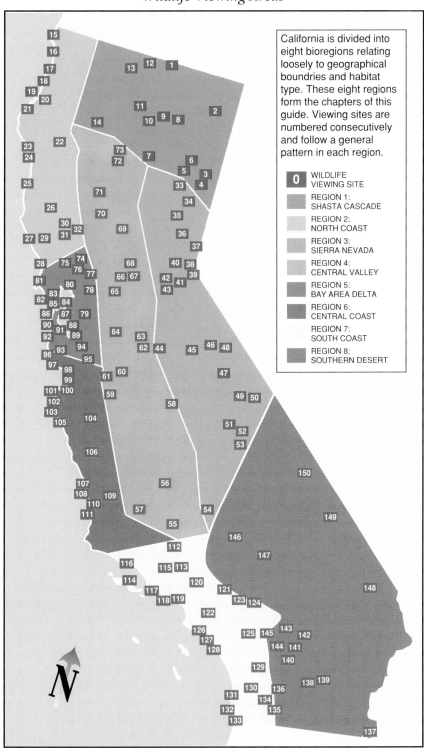

California is divided into eight bioregions relating loosely to geographical boundries and habitat type. These eight regions form the chapters of this guide. Viewing sites are numbered consecutively and follow a general pattern in each region.

0 WILDLIFE VIEWING SITE

REGION 1: SHASTA CASCADE

REGION 2: NORTH COAST

REGION 3: SIERRA NEVADA

REGION 4: CENTRAL VALLEY

REGION 5: BAY AREA DELTA

REGION 6: CENTRAL COAST

REGION 7: SOUTH COAST

REGION 8: SOUTHERN DESERT

SHASTA CASCADE

The Water Supply

California's water supply follows a complex cycle. Clouds pick up moisture from the ocean, move inland, and release rain or snow. Some of the moisture recharges the aquifer and lakes. Some runs off into streams that join the Sacramento River, flow through the Delta into San Francisco Bay, and reenter the ocean, where the cycle is repeated. This natural pattern has been altered because much of California's water supply is drawn from this region, where dams and reservoirs store water. Water is vital to wildlife. Rain nourishes vegetation that offers food, cover, or nesting habitat. Spring floods clean out stream silt and debris, and fill lakes and river floodplains, pro-viding habitat to Pacific Flyway migrants. The same rivers are highways for salmon and steel-head, which leave the ocean and swim upriver to spawn. When dams, diversions, and reservoirs reduce streamflow or eliminate seasonal wetlands, the effects on wildlife can be profound.

Left: salmon
Upper Right: bald eagle
Lower Right: mallards
Illustration: Del Rio-Price and Charly Price

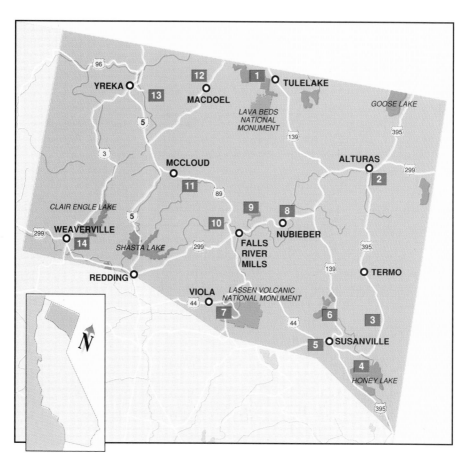

1 Klamath Basin National
  Wildlife Refuges
2 Modoc National Wildlife Refuge
3 Biscar Wildlife Area
4 Honey Lake Wildlife Area
5 Bizz-Johnson Trail/Susan River
6 Eagle Lake
7 Lassen Volcanic National Park

8 Ash Creek Wildlife Area
9 Big Lake/Ahjumawi Lava Springs
  State Park
10 McArthur-Burney Falls State Park
11 McCloud River Loop
12 Butte Valley Basin
13 Shasta Valley Wildlife Area
14 Lewiston Lake/Trinity River Hatchery

Description: Lower Klamath, the nation's first wildlife refuge, and Tule Lake are two of six Klamath Basin refuges. A patchwork of ponds, marshes, and farmlands shelter one million migratory waterfowl, with huge flocks of northern pintails, American wigeons, snow geese, and cackling Canada geese, the smallest species of Canada geese. At least 170 species breed here, including grebes, cinnamon teal, and threatened greater sandhill cranes. The two refuges claim the largest concentration of wintering bald eagles in the lower forty-eight states. The refuges are separated by Sheepy Ridge, high country used by birds of prey, pronghorn, and mule deer. Tule Lake shares a boundary with Lava Beds National Monument, where desert plateaus, rugged craters, and lava tubes and caves offer vastly different wildlife viewing.

Viewing Information: Excellent viewing opportunities for many of the more than 275 bird species. Look for white-fronted geese from September to April and snow geese from November to March. Many ducks also winter over. See bald eagles from December to March. Spring brings grebes and white pelicans, and pronghorn antelope are best seen in spring and summer. CALTRANS has an outstanding vista point on Highway 161, nine miles east of Highway 97. Excellent roads and auto tour.

Directions: From Highway 5, take Highway 97 north to Highway 161. Head east nine miles to Lower Klamath auto tour. To reach Tule Lake, continue on Highway 161 for eight miles to Hill Road. Turn south and drive four miles to visitor center.

Ownership: USFWS (916) 667-2231
Size: 86,500 **Closest Town:** Tule Lake

Bald eagles often roost near water, where they can feed on waterfowl and fish. Eagles mate for life, usually returning to the same nest, year after year. They are endangered because DDT and other toxins accumulated in their prey, causing thin-shelled eggs that broke during incubation.

ART WOLFE

Description: The rugged Warner Mountains rise dramatically above remote ponds,, wet meadows, and sage uplands along the Pit River. Redheads, gadwalls, hundreds of tundra swans, and other waterfowl gather on extensive marshes; shorebirds fan out on mudflats. Dense wetland vegetation hides secretive nesting species, including black-crowned night herons, and Virginia and sora rails. Greater sandhill cranes perform elaborate spring courtship dances before nesting. Summer broods of Canada geese, cinnamon teal, willets, and others are mixed among white pelicans, great egrets, and white-faced ibis. Resident mule deer gather near headquarters and along the two-mile auto tour that encircles Teal Pond. Jackrabbits, cottontails, and muskrats are common, as are migratory songbirds.

Viewing Information: More than 230 bird species; seventy-six nest here. High probability of seeing waterfowl, shorebirds, and songbirds in spring and fall, including cranes. Good viewing of bald eagles in winter. Excellent birding near headquarters, on auto tour. South of Alturas, look for cranes on east side of Highway 395; pronghorn on west side in spring.

Directions: *From Highway 395 (Main Street) at south end of Alturas, turn east on County Road 56. Go .5 mile, turn right on County Road 115. Go one mile, turn left on entrance road to headquarters.*

Ownership: USFWS (916) 233-3572
Size: 6,280 acres   **Closest Town:** Alturas

The tundra swans' high-pitched whistling calls can be heard long before the birds appear. In the spring, high-stepping males arch their necks and extend their wings in an effort to impress a mate.   TOM & PAT LEESON

3 BISCAR WILDLIFE AREA

Description: This small, high desert lake tucked in an arid rimrock canyon attracts white pelicans, ospreys, and other water birds. Muskrats and marsh wrens inhabit wetland areas. Pronghorn and mule deer come to water near dawn and dusk during the summer. Surrounding junipers, rabbitbrush, and sage conceal chukars, sage grouse, and other upland bird species.

Viewing Information: Waterfowl viewing is excellent from spring through early fall; also good for osprey. Look for upland birds in spring and summer, and wading birds in summer. On drive to and from site, scan private wetlands for cormorants, and waterfowl. *ROUGH DIRT ROAD; IMPASSABLE WHEN WET. CALL FOR ROAD INFORMATION.*

Directions: *From Litchfield, drive twenty miles north on Highway 395. Turn west on Karlo Road. Cross railroad tracks to reach site, which is six miles from highway.*

Ownership: BLM (916) 257-0456
Size: 270 acres   **Closest Town:** Litchfield

4 HONEY LAKE WILDLIFE AREA

Description: Alkali-tolerant vegetation fringes this sprawling, shallow lake in the Great Basin Desert. Wetlands support many migratory birds, including snowy plovers and tundra swans. Shorebirds and Canada geese nest on man-made islands. Waterfowl and greater sandhill cranes nest on nearby grasslands or among marsh vegetation that also hides white-faced ibises. Threatened bank swallows nest in burrows along the Susan River. Sage uplands offer excellent winter and spring views of pronghorn.

Viewing Information: More than 200 bird species. Waterfowl, wading birds, and shorebirds are best seen in spring, though viewing is good in fall. Cranes perform courtship displays in April. Look for bank swallows and songbirds from March through July. Birds of prey are residents and bald eagles winter here. Good site for seeing beavers. *NO VIEWING WEDNESDAYS, SATURDAYS, AND SUNDAYS DURING WATERFOWL HUNTING SEASON.*

Directions: *From Highway 395, about eighty miles north of Reno, turn east on County Road A3 (Lake Crest Road). Drive about eight miles to Standish and turn right on Highway 395. Drive six miles to County Road 305 (Mapes Lane) and turn right. Drive two miles to County Road 318 (Fish and Game Road) and turn left. Go one mile to Department of Fish and Game headquarters.*

Ownership: DFG (916) 254-6644
Size: 7,840 acres   **Closest Town:** Susanville

Description: This twenty-five-mile trail parallels a river canyon through three bioregions—the Sierra Nevada, Cascade Range, and Great Basin Desert. The trail, linking Susanville and Westwood, follows an old railroad grade through tunnels and across bridges and skirts the Susan River for sixteen miles. It moves from high desert, through south-facing grasslands and oak woodlands, past north-facing firs and pines, and ends in a dense pine and cedar forest. River vegetation shelters many birds, from belted kingfishers and hooded orioles to calliope hummingbirds and canyon wrens. Brushy dams and grassy mounds along the river are evidence of beavers and muskrats. Watch for turkey vultures, American kestrels, great horned owls, and other raptors. Patient observers may see bats, raccoons, porcupines, coyotes, even black bears.

Viewing Information: Nearly 100 bird species. Songbirds best seen in spring and fall, though summer is also good. Look for birds of prey, deer, predators, and aquatic mammals year-round, mostly mornings and evenings. Many butterflies. Nine access points to trail; travel on foot, horseback, bicycle, or cross-country skis.

Directions: In Susanville. Take Highway 36 (Main Street) to South Lassen Street and turn south. Drive four blocks to the Hobo Camp trailhead.

Ownership: BLM (916) 257-0456; USFS
Size: 10,000 acres   **Closest Town:** Susanville

Its name means "one who rises in anger", an apt description of how an angry porcupine appears when it raises its quills in defense. Porcupines are normally nocturnal; trees with missing bark or neatly chewed limbs are the best evidence of their presence.

WILLIAM R. RADKE

6 EAGLE LAKE

Description: Pine and cedar forests cloak the south shore of this large lake set beneath the Sierra Nevada and Cascade Range, while juniper and sage dominate the north side. A species unique to the lake, Eagle Lake rainbow trout, attracts western grebes, buffleheads, and many diving ducks; cormorants, terns, ospreys, and endangered bald eagles do their fishing from the skies. White pelicans, cinnamon teal, and other waterfowl feed near shore, as do many shorebirds. Quiet marshy areas are home to egrets and muskrats.

Viewing Information: High probability of seeing waterfowl, shorebirds, ospreys, and deer from May to June and September to October; also good viewing in summer. Waterfowl perform courtship displays in spring. Look for bald eagles and trout April through December. Excellent car viewing.

Directions: *From Susanville, follow Highway 139 north for twenty-five miles to lake. Take County Road A-1 northwest for sixteen miles to south lake.*

Ownership: BLM, (916) 257-0456; USFS, (916) 257-2151)
Size: 28,000-acre lake   **Closest Town:** Susanville

7 LASSEN VOLCANIC NATIONAL PARK

Description: A rugged landscape of cinder cones, hot springs, and volcanic vents is softened by forests, meadows, lakes, and streams and crowned by 10,457-foot Lassen Peak. Fifty lakes attract Canada geese, redheads, and other waterfowl in summer. Crystal clear streams offer glimpses of American dippers, slate gray birds that "fly" underwater as they feed. Mule deer and upland birds inhabit high meadows. Anna's, rufous, and calliope hummingbirds summer in the forest among resident Steller's jays and Clark's nutcrackers. Yellow-bellied marmots and squirrels frequent the campgrounds.

Viewing Information: Watch for waterfowl from June through September. Summer visitors may see flycatchers, finches, and glimpse an occasional peregrine falcon or bald eagle. Deer, marmots, and squirrels are readily seen from May through September. Excellent roads; best viewing from 150 miles of trails. Visitor center at north entrance.

Directions: *Take Highway 36 east from Red Bluff or Highway 44 east from Redding.*

Ownership: NPS (916) 595-4444
Size: 106,372 acres   **Closest Town:** Mineral

8 ASH CREEK WILDLIFE AREA

Description: This major spring staging area for waterfowl has extensive fresh-water marshes, six meandering streams, seasonal vernal pools, and is set in a broad valley with spectacular views of Lassen Peak and Mount Shasta. The pristine 3,000-acre Big Swamp and other wetlands attract white pelicans, Ross' geese, and northern pintails. Marshes near Wayman Barn, a landmark built without nails, offer spring views of courting greater sandhill cranes, foraging shorebirds, and nesting muskrats. Rodents in the grasslands sustain several resident owl species. Swainson's hawks and bald eagles visit seasonally. Lava rock and junipers flank Pilot Butte, home to pronghorn and a strutting ground for sage grouse.

Viewing Information: Nearly 200 bird species. Abundant waterfowl, shorebirds, and wading birds in spring and fall. Look for greater sandhill cranes in spring and summer and cackling Canada geese in fall. Bald eagle watching is good in winter. Deer seen summer and fall; pronghorn from spring through fall. Spring wildflowers include the rare Mathias button celery. *SITE IS REMOTE, UNDEVELOPED.*

Directions: *From Redding, take Highway 299 east to Bieber. Continue east three miles on 299 to Department of Fish and Game headquarters.*

Ownership: DFG (916) 294-5824, (916) 225-2300
Size: 14,160 acres   **Closest Town:** Bieber

The daisy-like blooms of arrowleaf balsam root and other spring wildflowers add brilliant color to hillsides and meadows within Lassen Park's rugged volcanic landscape. GEORGE WARD

9 BIG LAKE/AHJUMAWI LAVA SPRINGS STATE PARK

Description: Isolated Big Lake, a PG&E fishing hotspot, is bordered by the grasslands, forested hills, and rugged lava flows of Ahjumawi State Park. The open water and adjacent fields draw heavy concentrations of geese, swans, and ducks; Canada geese, northern pintails, and others remain to nest. The shoreline and Tule Creek offer views of western pond turtles, garter snakes, and great blue herons; a heron rookery is located among the pines east of Crystal Springs. Pine and juniper forests shelter mule deer, coyotes, yellow-bellied marmots, and porcupines. Several springs flow from the surrounding lava fields, where junipers are topped by the aeries of nesting ospreys.

Viewing Information: *NO ROAD ACCESS TO STATE PARK; CAN ONLY BE REACHED BY BOAT.* Waterfowl viewing is excellent, spring through fall. Cackling Canada geese best seen in spring, white pelicans in summer. Look for swans and geese in winter. The heron rookery and ospreys are active during late spring and summer. Suckers spawn in lava springs. Be alert for rattlesnakes. Waterfowl hunting October to mid-January. Park map at Big Lake boat ramp.

Directions: *From Redding, take Highway 299 east to McArthur. Turn north on Main Street. Road becomes dirt past fairgrounds. Follow sign for McArthur Swamp; shortly after sign, take right fork of road, cross canal, pass through open gate, and drive three miles to lake.*

Ownership: DPR, (916) 335-2777; Pacific Gas & Electric, (800) 552-4743
Size: 10,000 acres   **Closest Town:** McArthur

Coyotes are common throughout the state, even inhabiting the outskirts of large cities. They are outstanding runners, can leap long distances, and are extremely vocal. Listen for them throughout the night, providing a rich chorus of barks, yelps, and mournful howls.

B. "MOOSE" PETERSON

10 MCARTHUR-BURNEY FALLS STATE PARK

Description: In a landscape of forests and lava flows, streams wind through lush riparian corridors, cascade down spectacular Burney Falls, then rush into Lake Britton. Black swifts and swallows nest behind and near the 129-foot falls. The canyon below shelters belted kingfishers, squirrels, skunks, and many songbirds. Double-crested cormorants, pied-billed grebes, and bald eagles fish the open lake. Great blue herons, mallards, and ruddy ducks feed near the oak-lined shore. Watch for owls, woodpeckers, and other species in the open, park-like forests.

Viewing Information: Over 130 bird species. Waterfowl watching is good from fall through spring. Look for swifts and swallows in summer. Bald eagles nest here. Small mammals are seen spring through fall. Patient, quiet bird watchers have best success. On Pacific Crest Trail. Park crowded in summer.

Directions: *From Redding, take Highway 299 east six miles past Burney to junction with Highway 89. Drive north on Highway 89 six miles to entrance.*

Ownership: DPR (916) 335-2777
Size: 768 acres   **Closest Town:** Burney

11 MCCLOUD RIVER LOOP

Description: This six-mile driving loop passes through chaparral and forests, skirts the McCloud River and offers views of two spectacular waterfalls and a fifty-acre riparian meadow. Ponderosa pines along the river hide squirrels, chipmunks, many songbirds, even an occasional black bear. Scenic Upper Falls shelters belted kingfishers and nesting American dippers. Mule deer, Cooper's and sharp-shinned hawks can often be spotted at Bigelow Meadow, a blue grouse haven in the spring.

Viewing Information: High probability of seeing songbirds in spring and fall. Look for birds of prey in spring and summer. Deer common in summer. Many reptiles, amphibians; spring wildflowers. Handicapped facilities at Fowler Camp. *DRIVING LOOP IS DIRT; IMPASSABLE IN WET WEATHER.*

Directions: *Take Interstate 5 north of Redding to Highway 89 and turn east. The driving loop begins five miles past the town of McCloud at Fowler Campground and returns to Highway 89 about eleven miles east of McCloud.*

Ownership: USFS (916) 246-5130
Size: 2,625 acres   **Closest Town:** McCloud

12 BUTTE VALLEY BASIN

Description: DFG's Wildlife Area and USFS's National Grasslands combine with private lands to offer ninety square miles of wetlands, sage flats, and farmlands, dominated by 3,000-acre Meiss Lake and sweeping views of the Cascades and Mount Shasta. Seasonally, waterfowl are abundant. Huge flocks of white-fronted and snow geese leave the wetlands to feed on private grain fields and pastures, areas that often include hundreds of foraging pronghorn. Rodents in fields draw Swainson's hawks, prairie falcons, and golden eagles; bald eagles work the lake and ponds. In the sage flats, watch the ground for burrowing owls, badgers, and the state bird, the California quail.

Viewing Information: High probability of seeing waterfowl, wading birds, greater sandhill cranes in spring and summer. Look for snow geese in spring. Birds of prey can be seen year-round; resident golden and bald eagles provide excellent viewing from February to May. Seventy pairs of nesting Swainson's Hawks, most active from April to August. Excellent car viewing; auto tour. National grassland sites offer campgrounds, handicapped-accessible restrooms. Watch for birds of prey on private lands near Shady Dell and Sheep Mountain roads. No trespassing please.

Directions: *On Highway 97, .5 mile south of MacDoel, turn west on Meiss Lake Road. Continue 5.1 miles to DFG's Wildlife Area. To see USFS's Butte Valley National Grasslands, turn at marked exits north of MacDoel on Highway 97.*

Ownership: DFG, (916) 398-4627; USFS, (916) 398-4391
Size: 34,000 acres   **Closest Town:** MacDoel

Pronghorn find safety in large numbers and vast, open country. They possess excellent vision and can spot danger as far as four miles distant. They are also the Western Hemisphere's fastest mammals, running at speeds of seventy miles per hour. Several pronghorn relocations have re-established herds in areas where they were native.

TOM & PAT LEESON

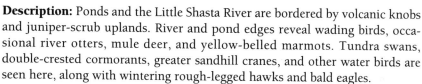

Description: Ponds and the Little Shasta River are bordered by volcanic knobs and juniper-scrub uplands. River and pond edges reveal wading birds, occasional river otters, mule deer, and yellow-belled marmots. Tundra swans, double-crested cormorants, greater sandhill cranes, and other water birds are seen here, along with wintering rough-legged hawks and bald eagles.

Viewing Information: Waterfowl watching is excellent in spring and summer; look for swans in winter. Wading birds can be seen year-round; cranes visit in spring and fall. Deer are common in winter. Marmots most active during spring and summer. Many resident predators, small mammals, raptors, upland birds. *A REMOTE, UNIMPROVED SITE.*

Directions: *From Interstate 5 at Yreka, take Highway 3 east eight miles to Montague. In town, take Ball Mountain/Little Shasta Road east 1.5 miles to entrance sign; turn right and continue .5 mile to DGF headquarters.*

Ownership: DFG (916) 225-2300
Size: 4,650 acres   **Closest Town:** Montague

14 **LEWISTON LAKE/TRINITY RIVER HATCHERY**

Description: The cold waters of this mountain lake downstream from Trinity Lake provide perfect habitat for rainbow, brown, and brook trout that draw ospreys, and golden and bald eagles. Marshes along fifteen miles of shoreline shelter wintering common mergansers, wood ducks, and other waterfowl, as well as resident herons, beavers, and river otters. Rushing feeder creeks offer views of American dippers, raccoons, and gray foxes. The conifer canopy hides northern orioles, Anna's hummingbirds, and other songbirds. Watch ospreys and eagles fish when salmon and steelhead spawn in the river below Lewiston Dam and at adjacent Trinity River Hatchery.

Viewing Information: High probability of seeing waterfowl in winter. Songbirds best seen in spring and summer. Spawning at riffles and hatchery offers excellent viewing: look for spring chinook from June to September and fall chinook from September to November. Steelhead run is fair, from January to March. Lewiston lake is on the Trinity Heritage Scenic Byway.

Directions: *From Redding, take Highway 299 west thirty-seven miles. Turn at sign to Trinity Dam/Lewiston Lake; after about 5.5 miles, at junction, continue straight to Lewiston Lake or bear right to hatchery and spawning riffles.*

Ownership: USFS, (916) 246-5130 or (916) 623-2121; USBR
Size: 3,600 acres   **Closest Town:** Lewiston

Wetland Ecology

Wetlands perform at least three important functions:

1) Wetlands sustain resident wildlife and migrants, such as Aleutian Canada geese and black brant, which seek specific wetlands each year.

2) Wetlands support complex relationships between plants and wildlife, called food chains and webs.

3) Wetlands act as natural filters. Microorganisms on underwater plants intercept nutrients, sediments, even pollutants, carried by streams. These are converted to new plant and animal life. At Arcata Marsh (Site 20), treated wastewater has been used for wetland restoration and fish aquaculture.

Upper Left: osprey
Lower Left: microorganisms
Right: California brown pelican
Illustration: Del Rio-Price and Charly Price

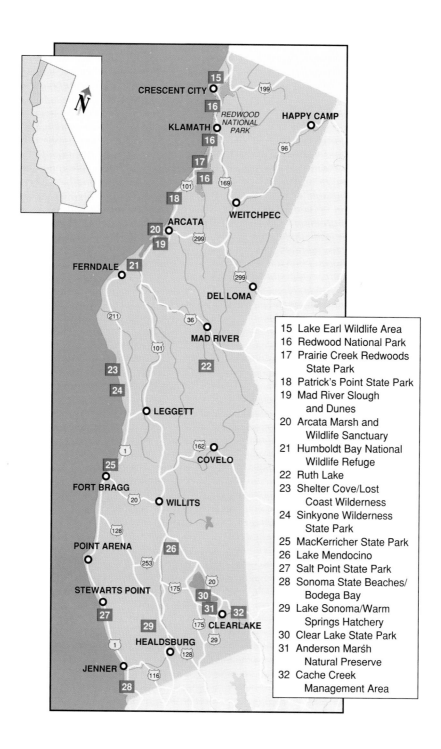

15 Lake Earl Wildlife Area
16 Redwood National Park
17 Prairie Creek Redwoods
    State Park
18 Patrick's Point State Park
19 Mad River Slough
    and Dunes
20 Arcata Marsh and
    Wildlife Sanctuary
21 Humboldt Bay National
    Wildlife Refuge
22 Ruth Lake
23 Shelter Cove/Lost
    Coast Wilderness
24 Sinkyone Wilderness
    State Park
25 MacKerricher State Park
26 Lake Mendocino
27 Salt Point State Park
28 Sonoma State Beaches/
    Bodega Bay
29 Lake Sonoma/Warm
    Springs Hatchery
30 Clear Lake State Park
31 Anderson Marsh
    Natural Preserve
32 Cache Creek
    Management Area

15 | LAKE EARL WILDLIFE AREA

Description: Isolated lakes Earl and Talawa are connected lagoons, bordered by salt and freshwater marshes and groves of Sitka spruce and red alder. Lake Earl is a staging area for 100,000 migratory birds, including Aleutian Canada geese and canvasbacks. Wetlands, riparian corridors, and forests attract many species, tundra swans, black-bellied plovers, peregrine falcons, and ruby-crowned kinglets. Lakes and creeks sustain river otters, muskrats, beavers, salmon, steelhead, and cutthroat trout. Harbor seals, sea lions, and endangered gray whales are visible offshore.

Viewing Information: More than 250 bird species, including eighty songbird species. Watch waterfowl and shorebirds from October through April. Aleutian Canada geese are seen in fall and spring. Canvasbacks are common in fall and winter. Look for bald eagles and peregrine falcons in winter. Wading birds, some ducks, and marine mammals are present year-round. Whales migrate from October through June. See area by car, on trails, by boat. Adjacent to 5,000-acre DPR project. Information at the DFG headquarters; tours. *HEAVY WINTER RAINS.*

Directions: *In Crescent City, drive north on Highway 101 to Northcrest Drive and veer left. Drive about two miles, then turn left on Old Mill Road. Follow signs to wildlife area.*

Ownership: DFG (707) 464-2523
Size: 5,000 acres   **Closest Town:** Crescent City

Aleutian Canada geese breed solely on the island chains between Alaska and Japan, and were nearly decimated after trappers introduced Arctic foxes to their nesting islands. Thousands of these endangered geese winter in habitat acquired for them at Lake Earl and in the Central Valley. CONNIE TOOPS

Description: This wildlife paradise encompasses thirty miles of coastline, inland streams, hills, and groves of coastal redwoods, the world's tallest trees and California's state tree. Sea lions and humpbacked and gray whales appear offshore; cormorants and other marine birds roost on coastal rocks. Low tides expose tidepools beneath sheer cliffs. Cinnamon teal, common mergansers, and other waterfowl gather at river estuaries, where shorebirds inhabit the tidal flats. Inland, streamside vegetation and mature forests sustain many songbirds. Oak woodlands are interspersed with prairies that attract Roosevelt elk, black-tailed deer, coyotes, and birds of prey. Black bears and small mammals seek the forest's cover. Rhododendrons and wildflowers bloom in late spring. Watch for bald eagles, peregrine falcons, and brown pelicans, all endangered.

Viewing Information: More than 300 bird species; about half are water-associated. Nearly 100 mammal and fifteen salamander species. High probability of seeing waterfowl in winter; songbirds and wading birds in spring and summer. Marbled murrelets and spotted owls found in old-growth forests. Marine mammals, sea birds, shorebirds, and birds of prey can be seen year-round. Good chance of seeing black bears during summer. *BE CAUTIOUS AROUND BEARS.* Look for Roosevelt elk from August to October. Whales migrate from October through June. Look for salmon and steelhead in streams. Excellent car viewing; fifty miles of roads. Many hiking trails. Three visitor centers. *VERY RAINY WINTERS.*

Directions: *Park headquarters located in Crescent City. Highway 101 runs through park between Crescent City and Orick. Many well-marked access points.*

Ownership: NPS (707) 464-6101
Size: 110,132 acres   **Closest Town:** Crescent City

In addition to abundant wildlife and towering redwoods, Redwood National Park is known for its outstanding rhododendron groves. The showy flowers thrive in damp, coastal forests, often alongside redwood sorrel and ferns.

CHUCK PLACE

17 PRAIRIE CREEK REDWOODS STATE PARK

Description: From fern canyons and redwood groves to stream-laced foothills and pounding surf, this scenic park has everything. Grasslands near Gold Bluffs Beach and Elk Prairie attract easily viewed Roosevelt elk all year. More than six fern species line sheer-walled Fern Canyon, home to American dippers, winter wrens, and Pacific giant salamanders. Lush Espa Lagoon sustains fish, waterfowl, even river otters. Dense redwood groves perched on ocean bluffs shelter resident marbled murrelets, small mammals, and songbirds. Marsh estuaries, barrier dunes, and sandy beaches extend for thirty miles and are a haven for water-associated birds.

Viewing Information: More than 260 bird species, many residents. High probability of seeing waterfowl and shorebirds fall through spring; songbirds in spring and summer. Marbled murrelets best seen during morning and evening flights in old-growth forests. Watch for black bears at dawn and dusk fall through spring. Azaleas and rhododendrons bloom in spring. Seventy-five miles of hiking trails; twenty miles for bicycling. Trail for the blind and excellent handicapped access. *HEAVY RAIN FROM NOVEMBER TO MARCH.*

Directions: *From Eureka, take Highway 101 north; continue six miles north of Orick to park entrance.*

Ownership: DPR (707) 488-2171
Size: 14,000 acres **Closest Town:** Orick

It's risky to promise excellent views of wild animals, but the Roosevelt elk at Prairie Creek are almost always in the meadow at the park entrance. Enjoy watching, but don't get too close: they can be aggressive during the rut or when their calves are young.

GARY KRAMER

18 PATRICK'S POINT STATE PARK

Description: A rugged wooded headland juts into the ocean, providing views of marine birds, sea lions, and gray whales. The forest resonates with birdsong; raccoons and rabbits move through the understory. Trails to beaches descend scrub-covered cliffs, offering views of offshore sea stacks with nesting black oystercatchers, pigeon guillemots, and pelagic cormorants. Rocks and tidepools at Palmer's Point, known as a favorite haul-out for harbor seals and sea lions.

Viewing Information: More than 160 bird species. High probability of seeing waterfowl and shorebirds from fall through spring, songbirds in summer, marine birds in winter. Whales can be seen year-round, but best viewing is during spring migration. Look for black-tailed deer in meadows. More than 150 spring-flowering plants. Excellent trails. *DON'T FEED RACCOONS OR BEARS.*

Directions: From Eureka, take Highway 101 five miles north of Trinidad. Turn west on Patrick's Point Drive.

Ownership: DPR (707) 677-3570
Size: 640 acres **Closest Town:** Trinidad

19 MAD RIVER SLOUGH AND DUNES

Description: A cooperatively-managed ecosystem encompassing seven habitat types. The Forest and Slough Trail skirts mudflats, tidal channels, and salt marsh, a haven for egrets, waterfowl, and twenty-five shorebird species. The path enters a pine and spruce forest favored by salamanders and gray foxes. Red alders and willows line Iron Creek, a stopover for grosbeaks, crossbills, and other songbirds. The trail crosses moving dunes, where Pacific tree frogs hatch in pockets of seasonal water, then ends at the ocean.

Viewing Information: Wading birds are abundant year-round. Look for waterfowl in spring and fall, songbirds in spring and summer, and shorebirds in fall and winter. Site is behind locked gate and is closed Tuesdays, Wednesdays, and Thursdays. *DUNE VEGETATION IS FRAGILE.*

Directions: From Highway 101, take Highway 255 (Samoa Blvd.) exit west. Drive three miles to Young Street (Manilla turnoff) and turn right.

Ownership: BLM; Louisiana-Pacific Corp.; TNC;
Redwood Gun Club a cooperator, (707) 822-7648
Size: 250 acres **Closest Town:** Arcata

20 ARCATA MARSH AND WILDLIFE SANCTUARY

Description: This 174-acre model restoration project on Humboldt Bay uses treated wastewater to restore and enhance wetlands and raise salmon and trout for local creeks. Three freshwater marshes, a brackish lake, and a small salt marsh attract more than 200 bird species, muskrats, and river otters. Dunlins and marbled godwits rest on loafing islands. The water draws cinnamon teal, ospreys, and endangered brown pelicans. Song sparrows and marsh wrens perch on marsh vegetation. Egrets and herons are conspicuous, while sora and American bitterns hide among the cattails. Field mice and shorebirds stranded by high tides attract northern harriers, peregrine falcons, and other birds of prey.

Viewing Information: Outstanding birding. Look for waterfowl, shorebirds, and wading birds from October through April. Many residents and rarities, such as Iceland gulls and oldsquaws. Peregrine falcons can be seen from September through March, during high tides; bald eagles winter here. Songbirds are abundant spring through fall. Coastal cutthroat trout and salmon are raised at nearby aquaculture project ponds. Many trails, bird blinds, benches, and interpretive displays.

Directions: *In Arcata. From Highway 101, take Highway 255 (Samoa Blvd.) exit and drive west to I Street; turn left and drive one mile to site.*

Ownership: City of Arcata (707) 822-5957
Size: 174 acres   **Closest Town:** Arcata

Dry grasses and cattails provide excellent camouflage for the American bittern, a wary bird that inhabits fresh and brackish marshes throughout the state. Bitterns hide by standing still, often pointing their bills toward the sky. During spring, listen for the male's booming call. GARY R. ZAHM

Description: California's largest eelgrass beds, located at the south end of the state's second largest bay, form a vital spring staging area for black brant; more than 10,000 can be viewed at one time. Resident harbor seals glide through open waters, weaving among northern pintails, tundra swans, and other waterfowl; seals haul out and bear their young on intertidal mudflats. Tidal flats also attract thousands of shorebirds, including western sandpipers, dunlins, curlews, and willets. American bittern and other wading birds feed along Salmon Creek and Hookton Slough; look for songbirds in adjacent grasslands. California's northernmost heron rookery is located on Indian Island. Humboldt Bay is also a spawning, rearing, and feeding area for clams, crabs, flounder, and other species.

Viewing Information: Waterfowl and shorebird watching is excellent from October through April. Wading birds, brown pelicans, and birds of prey can be seen year-round. Look for songbirds in spring. Refuge is undeveloped. Easy walking, some car viewing.

Directions: From Eureka, go south on Highway 101 for eleven miles. Take the Hookton exit. Turn right on Eel River Drive and turn left immediately on Ranch Road. Drive .5 mile to the refuge gate.

Ownership: USFWS (707) 733-5406
Size: 2,200 acres   **Closest Town:** Eureka

Tens of thousands of wintering black brant feed and rest in Humboldt Bay's shallow eelgrass beds. During high tides, they raft up in large groups in the bay and rest. As sandbars with eelgrass are exposed by the ebbing tide, they fly to these areas to feed and preen. GARY KRAMER

22 RUTH LAKE

Description: This slender lake bordered by ponderosas and firs is off the beaten path and a birding hotspot. An abundant fishery draws ospreys and bald eagles. Quiet bays shelter common mergansers, wood ducks, and other waterfowl. Warblers, vireos, and woodpeckers hide and nest in the conifers. Look for resident herons and river otters at the marshy end of the lake. Nearby oaks attract many birds, also large herds of black-tailed deer.

Viewing Information: More than 200 bird species. Waterfowl viewing is excellent in spring and fall. Songbirds are abundant in spring. Osprey nest in spring and remain through fall. Resident, nesting bald eagles can also be seen. Viewing by car, boat, in campgrounds; some land around lake is private. Highway 36 is winding and scenic; allow 1.5 hours for drive.

Directions: South of Eureka, from the junction of highways 101 and 36, take Highway 36 east for fifty-four miles. Beyond town of Mad River, turn on County Road 501 (Ruth Lake Road).

Ownership: USFS (707) 524-6233
Size: 14,000 acres   **Closest Town:** Mad River

23 SHELTER COVE/LOST COAST WILDERNESS

Description: Gulls, terns, pelagic cormorants, and bald eagles cruise over kelp beds at this protected cove. Offshore rocks attract common murres and pigeon guillemots. During spring and fall, phalaropes, turnstones, and other shorebirds seek Black Sands Beach. Tidepools near Point Delgada shelter purple sea urchins, red abalone, and other marine life. Harbor seals, Steller sea lions, porpoises, and whales often appear offshore.

Viewing Information: Except shorebirds, most species are visible year-round. Gray whale watching is excellent from December through March. Site access through the King Range, which shelters everything from rattlesnakes to elk. *STEEP, WINDING PAVED ROAD. WET WINTERS. DANGEROUS SURF.*

Directions: From Highway 101 near Garberville, follow signs to Redway and Shelter Cove. In Redway, turn west on Briceland Road. After about fourteen miles, you will reach Whitethorn/Shelter Cove junction; turn onto Shelter Cove Road. Continue eleven miles, following signs to the cove. Allow forty-five minutes for the drive from Redway.

Ownership: BLM (707) 822-7648
Size: Ten acres   **Closest Town:** Shelter Cove

Description: This unspoiled Lost Coast park is known for its dense forests, steep gorges, rugged coastline, and magnificent vistas. An arduous drive into park ends at Needle Rock Visitor Center, with views of a six-mile-long terrace often occupied by Roosevelt elk. The grasslands lead to steep cliffs flanked by tidepools and battered by surf. Pelagic cormorants and common murres nest in offshore rocks that are also popular haul-outs for harbor seals and sea lions. The Coast Trail meanders for twenty miles, passing streams, redwood groves, and primitive camping spots. Patient observers may see deer, foxes, porcupines, even a black bear or mountain lion. Watch for gray whales offshore.

Viewing Information: *FOR EXPERIENCED MOUNTAIN DRIVERS; NO TRAILERS OR RVs. ACCESS ROAD IS DIRT, RUGGED, STEEP, AND WINDING; ONE-LANE FOR SIX MILES WITH FEW PULLOUTS. CARS OKAY IN SUMMER; FOUR-WHEEL-DRIVE VEHICLES ONLY IN WINTER.* Roosevelt elk, harbor seals, shorebirds, marine birds can be seen year-round. Whale watching is excellent in winter and spring. Ospreys are common. Iris blooms in spring and summer. All viewing by trails. Hike-in camping only at established sites.

Directions: *From Highway 101 near Garberville, follow signs to Redway and Shelter Cove. In Redway, turn west on Briceland Road. After about fourteen miles, at Whitethorn/Shelter Cove junction, take road to Whitethorn. Pavement ends after you pass through Whitethorn. Continue on dirt road, straight through Four Corners intersection, to Needle Rock. About 1.5 hours from Redway.*

Ownership: DPR (707) 946-2311
Size: 7,400 acres   **Closest Town:** Redway

In flight, the common murre looks like a loon; on land, it looks like a penguin. The murre is named for the murring sounds made by the colony. Look for them in offshore waters and on coastal rocks.

ART WOLFE

25 MACKERRICHER STATE PARK

Description: Eight scenic miles of rocky coastline, beaches, and dunes combine with forests, grasslands, and a lake to offer tremendous habitat diversity. Extensive barrier dunes support endangered plants and a rare dune beetle. Tidepools sparkle along the rocky shoreline near Laguna Point, where offshore rocks attract American black oystercatchers and are a rookery for harbor seals. Coastal waters include an underwater park. Inglenook Fen, an unusual wetland, supports salamanders, rare insects, shorebirds, and five species of owls. Waterfowl and wading birds frequent Lake Cleone and Mill Creek. Look for cedar waxwings and other songbirds in spring.

Viewing Information: Nearly 100 bird species. Shorebirds, waterfowl, wading birds, raptors, harbor seals, and tidepool inhabitants can be seen year-round. Look for waterfowl in winter. Brown Pelicans, common murres, and ospreys seen spring through fall. Watch gray whales from December through March. Wildflowers bloom in spring. *TIDEPOOLS BEST AT LOW TIDE; DANGEROUS SURF. PLEASE DON'T DISTURB TIDEPOOLS OR SEAL ROOKERY.*

Directions: *From Fort Bragg, travel north on Highway 101 for three miles to park entrance.*

Ownership: DPR (707) 964-9112, (707) 937-5804
Size: 2,065 acres **Closest Town:** Fort Bragg

Harbor seals appear in coastal waters and bays along the entire length of California. They bask and breed on secluded rock outcroppings. The smallest disturbance sends them diving, where they can remain submerged for more than twenty minutes sometimes at depths of several hundred feet. ART WOLFE

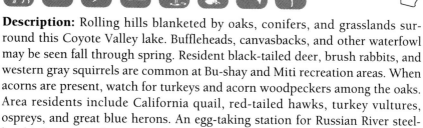

26 LAKE MENDOCINO

Description: Rolling hills blanketed by oaks, conifers, and grasslands surround this Coyote Valley lake. Buffleheads, canvasbacks, and other waterfowl may be seen fall through spring. Resident black-tailed deer, brush rabbits, and western gray squirrels are common at Bu-shay and Miti recreation areas. When acorns are present, watch for turkeys and acorn woodpeckers among the oaks. Area residents include California quail, red-tailed hawks, turkey vultures, ospreys, and great blue herons. An egg-taking station for Russian River steelhead is located at the south end of the lake, below Coyote Dam.

Viewing Information: Waterfowl and deer are best seen mornings and evenings. Boating may disperse waterfowl. Songbirds are common in spring. Visitor center. Steelhead spawning station open in winter and spring.

Directions: From the Highway 101/20 junction, there are two entrances to lake. On Highway 101 south of junction, take Lake Mendocino Drive. On Highway 20 east of junction, take Marina Drive.

Ownership: ACE (707) 462-7581
Size: 5,100 acres   **Closest Town:** Calpella; Ukiah

27 SALT POINT STATE PARK

Description: Stunning scenery and habitats range from an underwater reserve and rugged, seven-mile coastline to rolling hills and a forest of stunted cypress and pines. Sheer cliffs overlook rocky points, quiet coves, sandy beaches, and views of harbor seals, gray whales, and brown pelicans. Breeding pelagic cormorants gather at Stump Beach. Gerstle Cove, an underwater reserve, protects tidepools and other aquatic life. A grassy terrace draws northern harriers and black-shouldered kites. The forested coastal ridge shelters resident black-tailed deer, bobcats, and other mammals.

Viewing Information: High probability of seeing birds of prey in winter. Ospreys can be seen in summer, nesting between park and Stillwater Cove to north. Watch for gray whales in winter. Resident harbor seals give birth March to May. Tidepools are good year-round during low tides. *TIDEPOOLS ARE PROTECTED; DON'T DISTURB SEA LIFE AND PLEASE, NO COLLECTING.*

Directions: From Jenner, take Highway 1 north twenty miles to entrance.

Ownership: DPR (707) 847-3221
Size: 6,000 acres   **Closest Town:** Gualala

28 SONOMA STATE BEACHES/BODEGA BAY

Description: Ten miles of coastline encompass the Russian River estuary, a dozen beaches, and Bodega Bay Harbor. The estuary attracts thousands of waterfowl and shorebirds; streamside vegetation conceals ravens, wrens, and nesting ospreys. Harbor seals haul out on the sandspit, which extends south to their rookery at Goat Rock. From Shell Beach's tidepools to Bodega Head's whale-watching point, each beach attracts wildlife. Diverse habitats at Bodega Bay Harbor offer outstanding birding; a single day can produce sightings of loons, gulls, rails, and warblers; also look for pond turtles.

Viewing Information: Nearly 300 bird species; many residents. Excellent viewing of waterfowl, marine birds, shorebirds, songbirds in fall and spring. Ospreys can be seen from December to September. Marine mammals are seen year-round; look for harbor seal pups from March to June. Gray whales offshore from December to April. See tidepools at low tide. *PLEASE DON'T COLLECT OR DISTURB MARINE LIFE.*

Directions: From junction of Highway 1 and Highway 116 at coast, drive south on Highway 1 one mile to Goat Rock Road to estuary and Goat Rock State Beach. To see other beaches, resume travel south on·Highway 1. At Bodega Bay, take Bay Flat Road to harbor; the road dead-ends after three miles at Bodega Head.

Ownership: DPR (707) 865-2391
Size: Sixteen miles **Closest Town:** Bodega Bay

29 LAKE SONOMA/WARM SPRINGS HATCHERY

Description: Redwoods, firs, and oaks here sustain valley quail, acorn woodpeckers, California jays, small mammals, and many spring songbirds. Resident deer and feral pigs are visible in most clearings. Scores of coves and narrow fingers create habitat for egrets and cormorants. DFG's Warm Springs Hatchery spawns salmon and steelhead; watch for birds near the raceways.

Viewing Information: Raptors are seen year-round. Bald eagles are common in winter; look for peregrine falcons in spring and summer. Waterfowl and salmon are easily viewed in fall; steelhead in the spring. Viewing by boat, on foot, or horseback. Site includes an 8,000-acre wildlife area managed by DFG.

Directions: North of Healdsburg on Highway 101, take Dry Creek Road about ten miles north to visitor center and hatchery.

Ownership: ACE (707) 433-9483
Size: 19,000 acres **Closest Town:** Healdsburg

Description: This scenic park borders a natural lake at the foot of 4,200-foot Mount Konocti. With oaks and pines on high ground and willows and other riparian vegetation along watercourses, the area draws heavy concentrations of birds. There are outstanding shoreline views of the state's largest wintering population of western and Clark's grebes. Wood ducks nest in trees and herons hunt shallow lake and creek waters. Many varieties of fish flourish; several spawn here. Tree-bordered meadows offer views of black-tailed deer, valley quail, and an occasional bobcat, mink, or beaver. Wooded areas shelter great horned owls, northern flickers, and bushtits. There are active hot springs throughout the area.

Viewing Information: More than 150 birds species; many residents. Up to 500,000 wintering birds. Many spring nesting waterfowl and shorebirds. Watch courtship displays and floating nests of western grebes in winter and spring. Resident golden eagles. Peregrine falcons can be seen in winter; some nest. Pond turtles in sloughs and creeks. Come for fall colors and spring wildflowers. Visitor center.

Directions: *From Highway 29, take Kelseyville exit. In town, turn north on Gaddy Lane. At Soda Lake Road, turn right, following signs. Park is 3.5 miles from Kelseyville.*

Ownership: DPR (707) 279-4293
Size: 565 acres   **Closest Town:** Kelseyville

Look for bushtits in the small, outer branches of trees and shrubs. Families of bushtits often feed together, moving rapidly from shrub to shrub, calling constantly to each other. When roosting, they often huddle together to conserve body heat.

TOM & PAT LEESON

31 ANDERSON MARSH NATURAL PRESERVE

Description: This small preserve safeguards half of Clear Lake's tule marshes and supports everything from newts to white pelicans. Lush tules border the lake and offer food, cover, and breeding areas for fish, water-associated birds, and pond turtles. Opossums, minks, bats, and other mammals also use the marshes. Willows and alders along watercourses shelter bald eagles and hummingbirds. An oak woodland offers views of Cooper's hawks, cavity-nesting birds, black-tailed deer, and squirrels; lizards and rattlesnakes inhabit the forest floor. Grassy fields hide rodent runways and the spring nests of western meadowlarks and killdeer; they also draw hovering American kestrels and black-shouldered kites. There's a great blue heron rookery on site.

Viewing Information: Excellent viewing of waterfowl and songbirds from November through April. Western grebes, double-crested cormorants, and great blue herons can be seen year-round. Watch spring courtship and nesting of grebes. White pelicans best seen in winter. Osprey fish both summer and winter; bald eagles present from November through April. Quiet, patient observers can see many small mammals and songbirds.

Directions: *From the junction of highways 29 and 53 at Lower Lake, proceed north for .5 mile on Highway 53 to entrance.*

Ownership: DPR (707) 994-0688
Size: 540 acres   **Closest Town:** Lower Lake

Aerial acrobats, hummingbirds are able to hover in place and may even fly backwards, feats which make them unique among birds. The Anna's hummingbird (a female is shown here) commonly remains on the west coast during the winter.
JACK WILBURN

Description: This huge expanse of near-pristine land is cut by a perennial creek flanked by riparian vegetation, oak woodlands, and rugged, chaparral-covered hills. This is tule elk and bald eagle country. The creek's North Fork draws American wigeons and other waterfowl in the fall; streamside vegetation shelters great blue herons, belted kingfishers, even river otters. Golden and bald eagles often perch nearby, watching for brown trout. The oak woodlands and chaparral draw many spring songbirds and the hills are ablaze with wild-flowers, including the rare adobe lily. Turkeys inhabit the woodlands, usually within a mile of water. When creek flows are sufficient, view the area by raft. Watch for black bears along the creek.

Viewing Information: Tule elk and mule deer can be seen from October through April; look on hillsides, near cover. Bald eagles winter over from November through March. Look for river otters near entrance, north of Highway 20, under bridge. An undeveloped site. Please respect private property boundaries. Viewing on foot, horseback; have patience. Watch for elk one mile east of entrance, near gravel pit on Highway 20. Elk also seen near junction of highways 16 and 20.

Directions: From Clearlake Oaks on Highway 20, drive east eight miles to site entrance.

Ownership: BLM; DFG, (707) 462-3873
Size: 30,000 acres   **Closest Town:** Clearlake Oaks

Telltale slide marks on stream banks usually belong to river otters, known for their undisguised affection for fun. Special valves in the ears and nostrils block water when otters are submerged. Watch for these graceful, agile swimmers at Cache Creek and at Grizzly Island. ERWIN & PEGGY BAUER

SIERRA NEVADA

Moisture and Plant Communities

The Sierra Nevada (Spanish for "snowy range"), is a major watershed that collects, stores, and releases water into streams and lakes. Clouds carry moisture from the Pacific Ocean, releasing most of it on the lush, west side of the Sierra. The plant communities and wildlife here change with the elevation and level of precipitation. For instance, pileated woodpeckers are found in both deciduous and conifer forests; Williamson's sapsuckers require higher elevation forests. When clouds finally pass over the Sierra crest, rainfall decreases dramatically, creating a rainshadow. Eastern plant communities require little moisture. Pronghorn and sage hens inhabit the arid, lower elevations. Small, lightning-induced fires help rejuvenate Sierra Nevada forests. Notice the deer browsing on resprouting vegetation in the ash-covered foreground.

Lower Left: mule deer
Upper Left: pileated woodpecker
Right: pronghorn
Illustration: Del Rio-Price and Charly Price

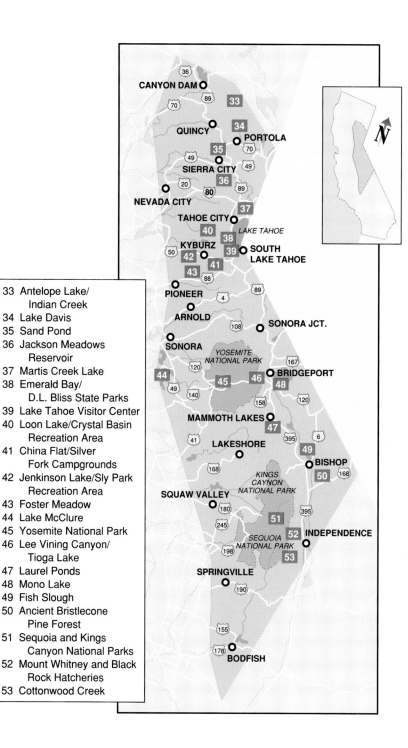

33 Antelope Lake/
   Indian Creek
34 Lake Davis
35 Sand Pond
36 Jackson Meadows
   Reservoir
37 Martis Creek Lake
38 Emerald Bay/
   D.L. Bliss State Parks
39 Lake Tahoe Visitor Center
40 Loon Lake/Crystal Basin
   Recreation Area
41 China Flat/Silver
   Fork Campgrounds
42 Jenkinson Lake/Sly Park
   Recreation Area
43 Foster Meadow
44 Lake McClure
45 Yosemite National Park
46 Lee Vining Canyon/
   Tioga Lake
47 Laurel Ponds
48 Mono Lake
49 Fish Slough
50 Ancient Bristlecone
   Pine Forest
51 Sequoia and Kings
   Canyon National Parks
52 Mount Whitney and Black
   Rock Hatcheries
53 Cottonwood Creek

CANYON DAM
QUINCY
PORTOLA
SIERRA CITY
NEVADA CITY
TAHOE CITY
LAKE TAHOE
KYBURZ
SOUTH LAKE TAHOE
PIONEER
ARNOLD
SONORA JCT.
SONORA
YOSEMITE NATIONAL PARK
BRIDGEPORT
MAMMOTH LAKES
LAKESHORE
BISHOP
KINGS CAYNON NATIONAL PARK
SQUAW VALLEY
INDEPENDENCE
SEQUOIA NATIONAL PARK
SPRINGVILLE
BODFISH

33 ANTELOPE LAKE/INDIAN CREEK

Description: More than a half-dozen creeks feed this remote lake. Pines and firs blanket the surrounding mountains and line the shoreline, where protected coves attract migratory waterfowl, including nesting mallards, cinnamon teal, gadwalls, and common mergansers. Western and Clark's grebes build floating nests on water milfoil at Long Point Cove. Canada geese and spotted sandpipers nest on several islands. Meadows along each creek are wet most of the year, an excellent place to see wood ducks, great blue herons, warbling vireos, warblers, even black bears. Broken-topped snags bear the nests of a half-dozen paired ospreys. Follow Little Antelope Creek upland to a series of brushy beaver dams; time the visit for evening to spot the beavers.

Viewing Information: High probability of seeing waterfowl April through November. Sandpipers and herons can be seen from May through July. Good raptor viewing year-round, including bald eagles; osprey are seen May through August. Beavers are active year-round. Wildflowers bloom from May through June. Drive in borders Indian Creek, with good wildlife viewing.

Directions: *From junction of highways 70/89, take Highway 89 north to Taylorsville turnoff. Turn toward Taylorsville, drive five miles, pass through town. Turn right on County Road 112. From here it is about twenty-seven miles to lake. After passing through Gennesse, road names may change; continue straight, following signs to lake.*

Ownership: USFS (916) 284-7126
Size: 1,500 acres   **Closest Town:** Greenville

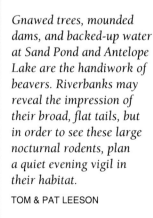

Gnawed trees, mounded dams, and backed-up water at Sand Pond and Antelope Lake are the handiwork of beavers. Riverbanks may reveal the impression of their broad, flat tails, but in order to see these large nocturnal rodents, plan a quiet evening vigil in their habitat.

TOM & PAT LEESON

34 LAKE DAVIS

Description: Trout spawn in four streams that feed this mountain lake bordered by meadows and pines. Canada geese nest on platforms or island mounds. A shoreline road offers summer views of white pelicans, sandpipers, and broods of Canada geese, western grebes, and mallards. Riparian vegetation lines creeks and meadows favored by mule deer and great blue herons. The pine forest hides many songbirds such as nuthatches and jays. Bald eagles visit the lake; watch snags on the east shore for a roosting pair.

Viewing Information: Waterfowl can be seen year-round; best viewing is from spring through fall. Look for tundra swans in fall. Bald eagle watching is excellent from March to May, and again in October and November. Ospreys frequent the lake from June to August. Occasional goshawk sightings. Deer are common in June and July. Watch bat flights in the evening.

Directions: *Take Highway 70 to Portola. Turn north on West Street and travel ten miles to lake.*

Ownership: USFS (916) 836-2575
Size: 560 acres   **Closest Town:** Portola

35 SAND POND

Description: The craggy Sierra Buttes form a backdrop for this serene pond. An interpretive trail follows fern-lined paths and crosses creek channels and marshes created by beaver dams. While the nocturnal beavers usually elude daytime visitors, the dams, gnawed trees, runways, and stream bank burrows reveal their presence. Wooden boardwalks lead across stretches of shallow, clear water, offering views of trout and summer mallard broods. The forest hides hairy woodpeckers and many songbirds.

Viewing Information: Site offers a closeup look at beaver activity and its impact on ecological processes. Observe beavers at night, spring through fall. Songbird viewing is fair, spring and summer. Heavy winter snow.

Directions: *From Sierra City/Highway 49, drive east five miles on Highway 49 to Gold Lake Highway at Bassett's Station and turn left. Go one mile, take Sardine Lake turnoff. Continue about .5 mile to Sand Pond.*

Ownership: USFS (916) 288-3232
Size: Ten acres   **Closest Town:** Sierra City

36 JACKSON MEADOWS RESERVOIR

Description: Aspen and lodgepole pine flank the rocky slopes surrounding this high, isolated mountain lake. The lake offers good summer views of broods of Canada geese and mergansers; mallards, green-winged teal, and a handful of shorebird species also visit in summer. More than fifty resident bird species, ranging from brown creepers to American dippers; these, like the resident mountain quail and blue grouse, are hard to spot. Several meadows offer good evening views of mule deer. Resident sharp-shinned hawks and Cooper's hawks fly low over the forested slopes; bald eagles visit in the late fall.

Viewing Information: Due to heavy snow, viewing here is restricted to summer and fall. Lakeshore is rugged with no trails. Many roads and pullouts for car viewing. Fall colors are outstanding; also wildflowers in spring. On the drive to the reservoir, watch wet meadows for deer and other wildlife.

Directions: From Truckee, take Highway 89 north for about fifteen miles. Turn left on Jackson Meadows Road and continue west for seventeen miles to reservoir.

Ownership: USFS (916) 265-4531
Size: 980 acres   **Closest Town:** Truckee

37 MARTIS CREEK LAKE

Description: Located on the east side of the Sierra crest, this lake is bordered by meadows, rolling sage-covered hills, and dense conifer forests. The reservoir supports threatened Lahontan cutthroat trout and attracts Canada geese and other waterfowl. Creeks shelter western wood peewees, nuthatches, and chickadees. Raccoons and golden-mantled ground squirrels appear near campgrounds. From here, in the mornings and evenings, watch the "edges"—where the forest, lake, and meadows meet—for browsing mule deer, soaring red-tailed hawks, and coyotes on the hunt.

Viewing Information: Heavy winter snow; viewing from spring through fall only. Alpine wildflowers in spring, summer. Songbird and predator viewing require patience and quiet.

Directions: From Highway 80, take Central Truckee exit. In town, turn southeast on Highway 267, toward Lake Tahoe. Drive three miles to Martis Creek Lake turnoff.

Ownership: ACE (916) 639-2342
Size: 1,800 acres   **Closest Town:** Truckee

Description: Two adjacent parks linked by trails are located in a spectacular alpine setting above one of the world's largest high-elevation lakes. Eagle Falls cascades into Emerald Bay against a backdrop of Lake Tahoe; watch here for soaring ospreys. Rock outcroppings and conifer forests line six miles of shore-line, where the Rubicon Trail leads to protected coves and views of common mergansers, pied-billed grebes, and mallards. The path weaves among pines, firs, and cedars, habitat for juncos, western tanagers, and white-headed and pileated woodpeckers. Squirrels and chipmunks are common; patient observers may see coyotes and pine martens, or bats, at dusk. Fall colors are covered by a mantle of winter snow, when snowshoe hares and bald eagles visit. Wild-flowers bloom just as Canada geese arrive to nest on Fannette Island.

Viewing Information: Moderate probability of seeing waterfowl, birds of prey, and songbirds in spring and summer. Winter offers views of eagles, pine martens, and lots of tracks. Nature center at nearby Sugar Pine State Park. Parks are crowded in summer.

Directions: *From Tahoe City, drive seventeen miles south on Highway 89 to D.L. Bliss State Park entrance. Continue four miles on Highway 89 to Emerald Bay State Park entrance.*

Ownership: DPR (916) 525-7277
Size: 1,830 acres   **Closest Town:** South Lake Tahoe

Pine martens are richly-furred cousins of the skunk, badger, and mink. They are agile climbers, spend much of their time in trees, and are active early in the morning or late in the afternoon. Inquisitive martens have been coaxed from their dens in trees or fallen logs by the sounds of squeaking mice. BEVERLY F. STEVENSON

39 LAKE TAHOE VISITOR CENTER

Description: Small but bountiful, this wet meadow bordered by creeks, forests, and beaches has a half-dozen trails highlighted by interpretive displays. Douglas squirrels and mule deer move among Jeffrey pines that shelter dark-eyed juncos, western tanagers, and hairy woodpeckers. Conifers and aspens give way to Taylor Creek Meadow, a grassy wetland crossed by the Rainbow Trail. Boardwalks and bridges offer views of ospreys and coyotes, also ponds with beaver dams. Boardwalks lead to a stream profile chamber with underwater views of trout, aquatic life, and, in fall, spawning kokanee salmon colored a brilliant red. Yellow-headed blackbirds perch among the cattails at Pope Marsh, where there are nesting platforms for Canada geese. The marsh and adjacent lakeshore beach offer views of mallards, western gulls, and the lake's largest concentration of wintering bald eagles.

Viewing Information: Viewing probability is high for waterfowl and gulls from spring through fall; moderate for songbirds, osprey, deer, and coyotes. Rainbow and brown trout can be seen in spring and summer; kokanee salmon run in the fall. Beavers sometimes seen on summer evenings. Annual Kokanee Salmon Jamboree. Visitor center. Wildlife viewing deck. Paved trail; excellent handicap access.

Directions: *From South Lake Tahoe and junction of highways 50 and 89, take Highway 89 north 3.5 miles. Turn right to entrance.*

Ownership: USFS (916) 573-2600
Size: Fifty acres   **Closest Town:** South Lake Tahoe

The coloration of kokanee salmon turns from silver to a brilliant red-orange in the fall as they prepare to spawn. The stream profile chamber at the Lake Tahoe visitors center offers a closeup view of this autumn wildlife spectacle. It's an easy hike to the chamber on a paved trail with boardwalks, interpretive displays, and excellent wildlife viewing. KEN MIRELL

40 LOON LAKE/CRYSTAL BASIN RECREATION AREA

Description: Loon Lake is one of five Crystal Basin reservoirs at the edge of Desolation Wilderness. Rocky outcroppings and forests offer glimpses of towhees, vireos, warblers, five woodpecker species, and occasional mountain quail and blue grouse. Yellow-bellied marmots sun themselves on rocks; mule deer, squirrels, and chipmunks are never far from cover. Snags serve as perches for ospreys, golden eagles, and other birds of prey. Quiet coves offer good views of loons, common mergansers, and Canada geese.

Viewing Information: High probability of seeing waterfowl, songbirds, woodpeckers, and deer in spring and summer; also uncommon birds, such as green-tailed towhees. Upland birds, birds of prey, small mammals, and black bears also present spring and summer. Crystal Basin is 75,000 acres. Gerle Creek has handicap accessible trail. Excellent viewing at Union Valley spring and fall. *GOOD PAVED ROAD, WINDING; WATCH FOR LOGGING TRUCKS.*

Directions: *From Pollock Pines, take Highway 50 east eight miles. Turn north on Icehouse Road and drive thirty miles to Loon Lake.*

Ownership: USFS (916) 644-2349
Size: 1,500 acres   **Closest Town:** Pollock Pines

41 CHINA FLAT/SILVER FORK CAMPGROUNDS

Description: Two campgrounds with remnant old-growth forests are located on the Silver Fork of the American River. Chipmunks, ground squirrels, and mule deer pass through camps. Northern flickers, Wilson's warblers, and common poorwills inhabit the wooded canopy. Evening campfires may illuminate eyes that belong to black bear, coyotes, or raccoons. Spotted, flammulated, saw-whet, and long-eared owls, also bats, appear in the night forest. The pristine river's vegetation hides Audubon's warblers and spotted sandpipers.

Viewing Information: Owls, woodpeckers, songbirds, bear, deer, and small mammals can be seen during spring and summer. Also look for bats and coyotes. Interpretive talks by naturalist in summer. Wildlife viewing here requires patient observation.

Directions: *From Highway 50 just south of Kyburz, take Silver Fork turnoff east. Drive three miles to China Flat; Silver Fork is five miles beyond.*

Ownership: USFS (916) 644-2324
Size: Twenty-eight acres   **Closest Town:** Kyburz

42 JENKINSON LAKE/SLY PARK RECREATION AREA

Description: Wildlife is abundant at this forested lake nestled in a foothill transition zone. Manzanita and mountain misery form dense thickets that attract black-tailed deer, mourning doves, and California quail, the state bird. A mixture of oaks, firs, pines, and cedars provides prime habitat for squirrels, skunks, porcupines, and dozens of bird species, including wrentits, Nashville warblers, black-headed grosbeaks, and pileated woodpeckers. Shoreline offers views of spotted sandpipers, rough-winged swallows, and yellow-legged frogs. Lake coves shelter buffleheads, common goldeneyes, grebes, and American coots. Sharp-shinned hawks, ospreys, and bald eagles can be viewed from scenic stops along an eight-mile trail that follows the shoreline.

Viewing Information: 135 bird species; fifty are common. Waterfowl are seen from fall through spring; also watch for deer above road, between Arrowhead and Stonebreakers camps. Songbirds are best seen in spring and summer; look for them early in morning where creeks enter lake. High probability of seeing birds of prey through winter and spring. Small mammals are seen year-round. Self-guided nature trails. Horse trail around lake. Tours by reservation.

Directions: *From Highway 50 at Pollock Pines, take Sly Park Road south 4.5 miles to park entrance.*

Ownership: USBR (916) 644-2545
Size: 2,000 acres   **Closest Town:** Pollock Pines

The California quail was named the state bird because it is widespread throughout the state. These gregarious birds forage in large coveys and, if frightened, scatter and race wildly on the ground before angling off in flight. Listen for the whirring sound of their wings.

ART WOLFE

43 FOSTER MEADOW

Description: The Middle Fork of the Cosumnes River meanders through this lush, wet meadow. Small pools fringed with summer wildflowers sustain mountain yellow-legged frogs. Summer grasses nourish deer and their fawns and hide long-tailed weasels searching for mice. Conifers shelter many birds, including woodpeckers, Wilson's warblers, and blue grouse. Watch for northern goshawks, identified by their bold white eyebrows and long, banded tails.

Viewing Information: Woodpeckers and long-tailed weasels may be seen in spring and fall. Deer, blue grouse, and songbirds are best seen in summer. Look for goshawks in spring and summer. A short walk to meadow. *SITE IS UNIMPROVED AND REMOTE. ROADS PASSABLE JUNE TO OCTOBER. WATCH FOR LOGGING TRUCKS.*

Directions: From junction of Highway 88 and Emigrant Trail, take Highway 88 west 4.5 miles to Foster Meadow sign and turn right. Road becomes dirt. Continue straight about one mile to Foster Meadow parking area.

Ownership: USFS (916) 622-5061
Size: Forty acres   **Closest Town:** Pioneer

44 LAKE MCCLURE

Description: The Merced River flows west from Yosemite and collects behind Exchequer Dam, forming two connected lakes thirty-three miles long. The towering, rock-filled dam creates tremendous updrafts ridden year-round by soaring golden eagles, red-tailed hawks, prairie falcons, and turkey vultures. Resident ospreys and wintering bald eagles appear at downstream hatcheries or wherever trout and bass are planted in the lake. Numerous coves and inlets shelter grebes, mergansers, wood ducks, and mallards, some of which are residents. Jays and nuthatches appear in the surrounding oak woodlands, along with black-tailed deer and occasional feral burros. Poppies, lupines, and lilies create a mantle of spring color on the hills.

Viewing Information: Many birds of prey are seen year-round; watch bald eagles in winter. Waterfowl best seen in fall. High probability of seeing black-tailed deer in summer and fall, especially near Barrett Cove. Wild burros also at cove summer mornings. Car viewing, short trails.

Directions: From Modesto, travel east on Highway 132 for thirty-eight miles. Turn south on Merced Falls Road. Drive five miles, then turn east on Barrett Cove Road. Proceed two miles to lake.

Ownership: Merced Irrigation District (209) 378-2521
Size: 7,000 acres   **Closest Town:** Snelling

45 YOSEMITE NATIONAL PARK

Description: This world-famous park brims with outstanding scenery and habitat. Towering peaks, sheer cliffs, spectacular water falls, vast meadows, hundreds of lakes, crystal-clear streams, and giant sequoias form a pristine wilderness that shelters nearly 250 bird species, eighty mammal species, twenty-nine types of reptiles and amphibians, and 1,400 species of flowering plants. Of these, bald eagles, peregrine falcons, great gray owls, wolverines, red fox, and California bighorn sheep are endangered. The park includes Tuolumne Meadows, the largest subalpine meadow complex in the world, as well as groves of ancient sequoias, some more than 2,500 years old. Most of the park is designated wilderness with 360 miles of paved roads and 800 miles of trails.

Viewing Information: *PARK IS EXTREMELY CROWDED BETWEEN MEMORIAL DAY AND LABOR DAY.* Look for golden-mantled ground squirrels, raccoons, coyotes, mule deer, golden eagles, band-tailed pigeons, Steller's jays, and acorn woodpeckers year-round. Western tanagers, black-headed grosbeaks, white-throated swifts, other songbirds are seen in spring and summer. Black bears sometimes seen from spring through fall. Watch for peregrine falcons in Yosemite Valley. Visitor center, tours. On Pacific Crest Trail.

Directions: *From Manteca and Interstate 5, take Highway 120 east to park. From Merced, take Highway 140 east. From Fresno, take Highway 41 north.*

Ownership: NPS (209) 372-0200
Size: 761,757 acres **Closest Town:** Mariposa

If left undisturbed, black bears might all be as unthreatening as this contented, cinnamon-colored fellow. Black bears can be a nuisance at popular camping spots, such as Yosemite or Prairie Creek (site seventeen in this book), where bears frequently appear to plunder carelessly-stored foods.

ART WOLFE

Description: This glacier-carved subalpine lake and canyon are located on the highest paved road in California. Watch for wildlife throughout the steep-walled canyon, especially California bighorn sheep. Vegetation along a meandering creek shelters Clark's nutcrackers, rock wrens, and occasional bobcats. Tioga Lake attracts Caspian's terns, California gulls, spotted sandpipers, and other shorebirds. A wet meadow offers views of hunting red-tailed hawks, yellow-bellied marmots, and spectacular spring wildflowers. The adjacent forest hides blue grouse, coyotes, pikas, and badgers.

Viewing Information: Highway 120 is a national forest scenic byway. ROADS IMPASSABLE IN WINTER. High probability of seeing shorebirds, gulls, small mammals from April through October. Songbirds are seen from May through August. Birds of prey appear year-round. Bighorn sheep are well-camouflaged and elusive. In spring and fall, stop at pullout 5.5 miles from Lee Vining; look north, near springs, for bighorn.

Directions: From Lee Vining, drive west on Highway 120 for 5.5 miles to pull-out; continue 6.5 miles to lake.

Ownership: USFS (619) 647-6525
Size: 5,000 acres   **Closest Town:** Lee Vining

Description: These cooperatively managed ponds and wetland were developed with treated wastewater. The ponds, in an otherwise arid setting, are a magnet for migratory waterfowl and shorebirds. Mallards, cinnamon teal, ring-necked ducks, Canada geese, avocets, and killdeer are common, with several breeding species. Great blue herons are conspicuous, but look for sora—the most common of rails—hiding among marsh vegetation. Resident prairie falcons and golden eagles share the skies with wintering rough-legged hawks. The open sage flats attract sage thrashers, sage sparrows, and sage hens and offer views of migratory deer, often 300 at a time.

Viewing Information: *ROAD IMPASSABLE IN WINTER.* Waterfowl, shorebirds, and songbirds are seen from May through November. Deer are common in May, September, and October.

Directions: From Bishop or Bridgeport, take Highway 395 to Convict Lake exit. Drive .2 mile and turn right on dirt road; continue two miles to pond.

Ownership: USFS (619) 924-5500
Size: 100 acres   **Closest Town:** Mammoth Lakes

48 MONO LAKE

Description: Set in the high desert beneath snow-capped peaks, this vast inland sea is more than 700,000 years old. The lake is dotted with delicate calcium-carbonate knobs and spires called tufa. Brine shrimp and flies thrive in water that is 2.5 times as salty and eighty times as alkaline as seawater, providing a feast for seventy species of migratory birds, including nearly one million eared grebes, huge flocks of killdeer, and Wilson's and red-necked phalaropes. The eastern shore is a major nesting area for snowy plovers and the nesting islands attract 50,000 California gulls, their largest rookery in the state. Area is a Western Hemisphere Shorebird Reserve Network site.

Viewing Information: *DO NOT DAMAGE OR COLLECT TUFA. REMAIN ONE MILE AWAY FROM NESTING ISLANDS FROM APRIL 1 THROUGH AUGUST 1.* High probability of seeing gulls and plovers from April to October. Waterfowl, shorebirds, wading birds, and birds of prey in spring and summer. Look for phalaropes in July and August, eared grebes from August to October. Jackrabbits, Belding's ground squirrels, and coyotes are residents. Visitor center.

Directions: *Take Highway 395 just north of Lee Vining to vistor center.*

Ownership: DPR, (619) 647-6331; USFS, (619) 647-6525
Size: 17,000 acres   **Closest Town:** Lee Vining

A wind-ravaged bristlecone pine offers mute testimony to the forces of wind, water, and time. Some of the pines are more than 4,600 years old, making them among the oldest living things on earth. Look among their twisted limbs for featherlight chickadees or colorful violent-green swallows.

LEE MAN SIMMONS

49 FISH SLOUGH

Description: Three natural springs flow from volcanic cliffs and form a cooperatively-managed marsh-lined slough that is a sanctuary for Owen's pupfish and Owen's tui chub. These endangered fish are found on six acres of clear ponds at two locations. The two-inch pupfish are easy to recognize by their distinctive "start-stop" swimming style. Yellow-headed blackbirds, prairie falcons, green-winged teal, and black-crowned night herons are also seen here.

Viewing Information: High probability of seeing wildlife. Pupfish and wading birds can be seen year-round. Look for birds of prey year-round. Waterfowl and shorebirds are common in fall and winter. Songbirds appear in fall and spring. *CRITICAL FISH HABITAT; PLEASE DON'T DISTURB.*

Directions: *In Bishop, take Highway 395 north to Highway 6. Drive north on Highway 6 for 1.5 miles, turn west on Five Bridges Road. Drive about 2.5 miles. Shortly after the sand and gravel plant, turn right on Fish Slough Road. Go one mile, cross a cattle guard, and travel 5.5 miles to fenced pond. Marshlands will be on east side of road as you drive to pond.*

Ownership: BLM, (619) 872-4881; DFG, (619) 872-1171; Los Angeles Dept. of Water and Power, (619) 872-1104
Size: 400 acres   **Closest Town:** Bishop

50 ANCIENT BRISTLECONE PINE FOREST

Description: The steep, wind-ravaged White Mountains sustain many wildlife species amidst a forest of gnarled bristlecone pines, among the oldest living things on earth. Tree ring patterns indicate the oldest pine is more than 4,600 years old. The twisted branches of these dramatic, wind-polished trees become temporary perches for songbirds such as mountain chickadees, hermit thrushes, mountain bluebirds, and violet-green swallows. Clark's nutcrackers, pinyon jays, and ravens are common. Watch for golden eagles and American kestrels scanning the slopes for white-tailed jackrabbits, chipmunks, and other mammals.

Viewing Information: Excellent songbird viewing. Birds of prey and small mammals are also common. Schulman Grove has visitor center. Spectacular views. Summer best for viewing. *INACCESSIBLE NOVEMBER THROUGH APRIL. CARRY WATER FOR CAR AND FOR DRINKING.*

Directions: *From Highway 395 in Big Pine, take Highway 168 east thirteen miles to Westgard Pass. Turn north on White Mountain Road; go ten miles to site.*

Ownership: USFS (619) 873-2525
Size: 28,887 acres   **Closest Town:** Big Pine

51 SEQUOIA AND KINGS CANYON NATIONAL PARKS

Description: Two pristine parks encompass breathtaking scenery, from 1,500-foot chaparral and oak foothills to a granite wilderness that includes 14,495-foot Mount Whitney, the highest peak in the lower forty-eight states. Wildlife habitats include three river systems, alpine lakes, gushing waterfalls, rugged canyons, glaciated valleys, meadows deep in wildflowers, dense conifer forests, and groves of ancient sequoias. Black bears and mule deer feed in the meadows. California bighorn sheep can be spotted near Rae Lakes during summer and fall. Gray foxes, yellow-bellied marmots, and squirrels are common, as are aquatic garter snakes and western rattlesnakes. Golden trout inhabit the Little Kern River. The more than 200 bird species range from nuthatches to goshawks. The parks have been designated an international Biosphere Reserve.

Viewing Information: White-headed woodpeckers, Clark's nutcrackers, Cassin's finches are seen year-round. Songbirds are best viewed in spring, including western tanagers, lazuli buntings, and black-headed grosbeaks. Bears are common from May to November. Look for deer at middle elevations during summer, in foothills during winter. Wildlife viewing changes with elevation. Five visitor centers. Limited roads; 700 miles of trails. On Pacific Crest Trail. *DRIVE CAREFULLY, WINDING ROADS.*

Directions: *For Kings Canyon, take Highway 180 east from Fresno. For Sequoia, take Highway 198 east from Visalia.*

Ownership: NPS (209) 565-3341
Size: 863,710 acres   **Closest Town:** Three Rivers

California's state fish, the golden trout, is known for its exceptional color. Most of the state's golden trout eggs are taken from wild fish at Cottonwood Lake, then raised at fish-rearing facilities. Look for wild golden trout at Cottonwood Creek or in streams at Sequoia National Park.   B. "MOOSE" PETERSON

52 MOUNT WHITNEY AND BLACK ROCK HATCHERIES

Description: Self-guided tours of raceways and the seventy-five year old Mount Whitney hatchery offer excellent views of rainbow trout broodstock and spawning. A natural pond here shelters great blue herons, green-winged teal, wood ducks, and other birds. The fish eggs are reared at other facilities, including nearby Black Rock Hatchery, where fish can be viewed year-round. Black Rock's natural ponds there attract many birds, ranging from white pelicans and Caspian's terns to ospreys and western tanagers. Tule elk often graze near each hatchery, on either side of Highway 395.

Viewing Information: Mount Whitney spawning occurs from March to May and from late October through December. Wading birds and elk are seen year-round. Waterfowl and songbirds are common in spring.

Directions: *Mount Whitney: from Independence, take Highway 395 north one mile. Black Rock is eight miles northeast of Mt. Whitney on Highway 395.*

Ownership: DFG (619) 878-2272
Size: Fifteen acres   **Closest Town:** Independence

53 COTTONWOOD CREEK

Description: Cottonwood Creek winds through high-elevation pines, bordered by a willow-lined wet meadow. Excellent summer views here of California's state fish, the colorful golden trout. DFG spawns wild fish at Cottonwood Lake, a five-mile hike from the lake trailhead; most of the eggs are packed out on mules to rearing facilities. Creekside trails offer views of wild trout, brown creepers, mountain bluebirds, and other songbirds. Watch for golden-mantled ground squirrels, yellow-bellied marmots, even snowshoe hares. Golden eagles are common.

Viewing Information: *ROADS IMPASSABLE WINTER AND SPRING.* Watch spawning at lake from May through June. Birds of prey, songbirds, and small mammals are seen summer and fall. Occasional black bears. Horseshoe Meadows Trailhead, with camping, horse corrals, and handicap accessible restrooms, is two miles beyond site.

Directions: *From Highway 395 in central Lone Pine, go west on Whitney Portal Road for three miles. Turn south on Horseshoe Mountain Road, drive about eighteen miles to picnic and camping area bordering creek. Cottonwood Lakes Trailhead nearby.*

Ownership: USFS, (619) 876-5544; Los Angeles
Dept. of Water and Power, (619) 872-1104
Size: Twenty acres   **Closest Town:** Lone Pine

CENTRAL VALLEY

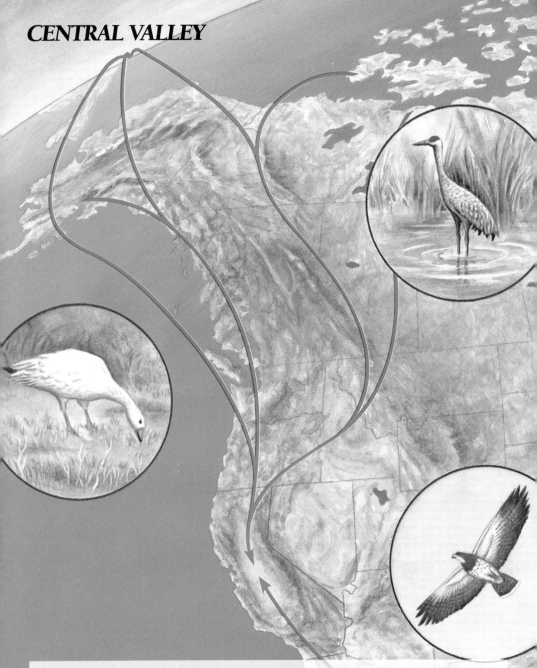

Connected to the World by a Flyway

The Central Valley's grasslands and wetlands, which support scores of resident species, are also connected to other countries by well-traveled highways in the sky. Millions of migratory ducks, geese, shorebirds, and other birds seek Central Valley wetlands each fall. Some, like cinnamon teal, stop briefly, then continue to Mexico. Swainson's hawks migrate from Mexico, seeking this valley to nest. Snow and Ross' geese winter in the Central Valley, then return north in the spring to breed. Ninety-one percent of the state's wetlands have been lost to agriculture, diversions, development, and other changes. Intensively-managed wetlands such as Gray Lodge Wildlife Area (Site 69), Sacramento National Wildlife Refuge (Site 70), and the Grasslands (Site 60), are crucial in maintaining centuries-old "landscape corridors" that link California to the rest of the world.

Left: snow goose
Upper Right: greater sandhill crane
Lower Right: Swainson's hawk
Illustration: Del Rio-Price and Charly Price

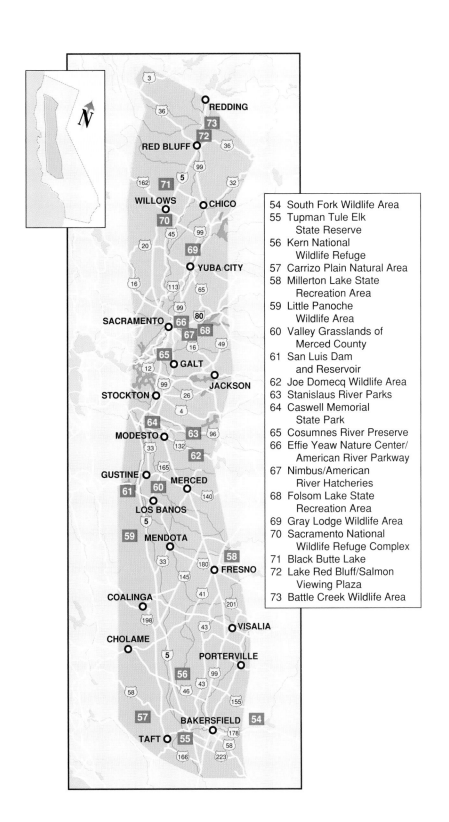

54 South Fork Wildlife Area
55 Tupman Tule Elk
   State Reserve
56 Kern National
   Wildlife Refuge
57 Carrizo Plain Natural Area
58 Millerton Lake State
   Recreation Area
59 Little Panoche
   Wildlife Area
60 Valley Grasslands of
   Merced County
61 San Luis Dam
   and Reservoir
62 Joe Domecq Wildlife Area
63 Stanislaus River Parks
64 Caswell Memorial
   State Park
65 Cosumnes River Preserve
66 Effie Yeaw Nature Center/
   American River Parkway
67 Nimbus/American
   River Hatcheries
68 Folsom Lake State
   Recreation Area
69 Gray Lodge Wildlife Area
70 Sacramento National
   Wildlife Refuge Complex
71 Black Butte Lake
72 Lake Red Bluff/Salmon
   Viewing Plaza
73 Battle Creek Wildlife Area

54 SOUTH FORK WILDLIFE AREA

Description: Only two percent of California's cottonwood and willow river forests remain; twenty percent of them are found on a fourteen-mile stretch of the Kern River. These outstanding river woodlands sustain the state's largest population of willow flycatchers and are breeding habitat for endangered western yellow-billed cuckoos. Great blue herons move among cattails joined by the woven nests of yellow-headed and tricolored blackbirds. Fish attract white pelicans, western grebes, occasional ospreys, and bald eagles, while muddy banks reveal the tracks of beavers, coyotes, black bears, even mountain lions. Woodpeckers, grosbeaks, wrens, and warblers seek the forest's sheltered canopy, where snags serve as perches for red-shouldered hawks and northern harriers. Mule deer are common and more than 100 species of butterflies have been sighted near Lake Isabella.

Viewing Information: More than 200 bird species. Uncommon migrants such as summer tanagers and yellow warblers. Birds of prey and waterfowl are seen year-round; waterfowl are best viewed in winter. Songbirds and butterflies are common in spring and summer. Look for cuckoos and flycatchers from June to September. Deer trails connect site to TNC's Kern River Preserve.

Directions: *From Bakersfield on Highway 99, take Highway 178 east forty-five miles. Continue driving past Lake Isabella about fifteen miles and turn north on Sierra Way. Drive four miles to wildlife area overlook and trailhead.*

Ownership: USFS (619) 376-3781
Size: 1,217 acres   **Closest Town:** Lake Isabella

Tule elk are native only to California. They were brought back from the brink of extinction by protection and successful relocation programs. This heavily-antlered bull grows a new set of antlers each year. Captive tule elk herds may be seen at sites 55, 60, 78, and 81.

WILLIAM GRENFELL

55 TUPMAN TULE ELK STATE RESERVE

Description: This natural grassland with managed ponds and marshes is tule elk habitat as it was a century ago. Watch impressive rutting displays of antlered bulls in fall, and wobbly calves in spring near the viewing areas or on guided tours. This unassuming site sustains four endangered species: the San Joaquin kit fox, San Joaquin antelope squirrel, Tipton kangaroo rat, and blunt-nosed leopard lizard; and the threatened plant, Hoover's woolystar. Nineteen others are candidates for federal listing, including western pond turtles, tricol-ored blackbirds, and northern harriers. Songbirds and birds of prey can be seen from the viewing area.

Viewing Information: Tule elk and birds of prey are seen year-round. Song-birds are best viewed in spring. Some protected species may be seen on guided tours. Viewing area is handicap-accessible. Visitor center.

Directions: *Near Bakersfield. From Interstate 5, take Stockdale Highway west 1.5 miles to Morris Road and turn left. Drive 1.25 miles to Station Road and turn right. Continue .25 mile to entrance.*

Ownership: DPR (805) 765-5004
Size: 956 acres   **Closest Town:** Buttonwillow

56 KERN NATIONAL WILDLIFE REFUGE

Description: The seasonal, managed marshes in this flat, alkali grassland draw northern pintails, redheads, teal, canvasbacks, grebes—nearly every species of dabbling duck and many diving ducks. Snowy egrets wade near tules and cat-tails that camouflage American bitterns and Virginia rails. Ringed-billed gulls mix among scores of shorebirds. Warblers, swallows, sparrows, and other songbirds perch among marsh plants. A half-dozen species of birds of prey watch marsh activity from aloft, including peregrine falcons. Artificial dens have been built for endangered San Joaquin kit foxes. Endangered blunt-nosed leopard lizards feed in the grasslands, mornings and evenings, between March and July.

Viewing Information: All bird viewing is from November to April, when wa-ter is present. Waterfowl watching is excellent in winter. Driving tour.

Directions: *At Lost Hills and Interstate 5, take Highway 46 east 5 miles to Corcoran Road and turn north. Drive 10.6 miles to refuge.*

Ownership: USFWS (805) 725-2767
Size: 10,618 acres   **Closest Town:** Delano

57 CARRIZO PLAIN NATURAL AREA

Description: This sixty-mile-long plain is the largest remaining sample of unique San Joaquin Valley ecosystems. Nearly 5,000 sandhill cranes winter at Soda Lake, a 3,000-acre alkali wetland that attracts scores of water-associated birds. Surrounding grasslands, alkali sink, and saltbush scrub shelter San Joaquin antelope squirrels and blunt-nosed leopard lizards, both endangered and often visible from the road. San Joaquin kit foxes and giant kangaroo rats, also endangered, venture from their burrows at dusk. The grasslands draw mountain plovers, western bluebirds, and horned larks. Isolated trees shelter Say's phoebes, western kingbirds, and Le Conte's thrashers. The area draws heavy concentrations of wintering birds of prey, including ferruginous hawks, northern harriers, prairie falcons, short-eared owls, and occasional bald eagles. Reintroduced tule elk and pronghorn antelope inhabit the foothills.

Viewing Information: More than 175 bird species, including eastern migrants. Excellent crane viewing October through February. Waterfowl and shorebirds are seen in winter. Songbirds and wildflowers appear in spring. Birds of prey, small mammals, and reptiles are residents. Visitor center open soon. *SITE IS VERY REMOTE AND UNIMPROVED. HOT IN SUMMER; NO WATER.*

Directions: *From Buttonwillow on Interstate 5, take Highway 58 west forty-five miles to Soda Lake Road. Turn south and drive fourteen miles to Painted Rock Visitor Center. Or from Paso Robles, drive south on Highway 101. Take Highway 58 east forty-five miles to Soda Lake Road; drive south to visitor center.*

Ownership: BLM, (805) 861-4236; DFG, (408) 649-2870;
TNC, (805) 545-9925

Size: 180,000 acres   **Closest Town:** Maricopa, Atascadero

The cat-sized, endangered San Joaquin kit fox is predominantly a night hunter, passing most of the day in an underground den. A mated pair may have thirty dens in a space of 600 acres. Less than seven percent of their original valley habitat remains.

E. TYLER CONRAD

Description: This large impoundment on the San Joaquin River was formed by Friant Dam. Ground squirrels and acorn woodpeckers inhabit oak-studded grasslands near north shore campgrounds. Watch closely here for bobcats, coyotes, and red-breasted and yellow-bellied sapsuckers. Look aloft for hunting golden eagles, northern harriers, and rough-legged hawks. Wintering bald eagles fish from shoreline trees, especially near MacKenzie and Winchell points. Many Canada geese winter here, among resident western grebes and American coots. Egrets and herons are conspicuous in the summer, wading in marshy areas created by the falling lake level.

Viewing Information: Waterfowl and wading birds are seen year-round. Songbirds appear in spring. Birds of prey and other predators are common in spring and fall. April brings wildflowers.

Directions: Take Highway 99 to the Madera exit and Highway 145. Follow Highway 145 twenty-two miles to lake.

Ownership: DPR, (209) 822-2332; USBR
Size: 13,000 acres   **Closest Town:** Friant

Description: This cattail-rimmed lake attracts migratory mallards, teal, rednecks, ring-necked ducks, and other waterfowl. Resident great blue herons wade along the shore. Atriplex, a low-lying shrub, provides nesting cover for tricolored blackbirds. Golden eagles and Cooper's hawks cruise over scrub-covered hills, watching for jackrabbits, deer mice, and Heerman's kangaroo rats. Prairie falcons nest in the white-stained bluffs across the lake. Roadrunners, meadowlarks, and mockingbirds are common. Follow the shore west to a gorge that hides Little Panoche Creek; look here for chukars, California quail, loggerhead shrikes, and spring migrants.

Viewing Information: Wading birds and some small mammals are seen year-round. Waterfowl are common in fall and winter. Look for birds of prey in winter and spring and songbirds in spring and summer. An undeveloped site managed by DFG; hike to see wildlife.

Directions: From twenty miles south of Los Banos, take Shields Avenue west toward Mercey Hot Springs. Drive 4.5 miles to site.

Ownership: USBR; DWR; managed by DFG (209) 826-0463
Size: 650 acres   **Closest Town:** Los Banos

Description: Native grasslands, manmade and natural ponds, streams, sloughs, and highly developed farm land form the central valley's largest block of wetlands and native grasslands. From 500,000 to one million Pacific Flyway birds winter here; the area, so important to shorebirds, has been designated a Western Hemisphere Shorebird Reserve Network site. Three driving loops offer easy car viewing, complemented by trails or driving tours at eight national wildlife refuges and state wildlife areas; *SEE MAP, OPPOSITE PAGE.*

North Loop: North of Los Banos on Highway 165, make a side trip to Los Banos WA's Buttonwillow Lake to see as many as 250,000 waterfowl at one time, including northern pintails, green-winged teal, gadwalls, Ross' geese, and white-fronted geese. Watch for herons, dunlins, western sandpipers, and scores of songbirds. Thousands of birds also gather at San Luis NWR, but the ponds are smaller and birds are dispersed. View captive tule elk from an observation tower. Visit Salt Slough WA, a developing marsh with many long-term restoration projects. Look for spring wildflowers and pools at Kestersen NWR and China Island WA, then drive past Sante Fe Road's private wetlands, with concentrations of waterfowl and shorebirds. Look for white-faced ibises and tundra swans.

South Loop: Flocks of northern pintails, northern shovelers, and green-winged teal gather on Mallard Road's intensively managed wetlands; up to 8,000 snow geese have been counted here. Marshy areas attract white-crowned sparrows, water pipits, and other songbirds. Watch pastures and fields for golden eagles, prairie falcons, and other birds of prey.

East Loop: Highways 152, 59, and Sandy Mush Road lead past concentrations of feeding shorebirds and hunting black-shouldered kites. Follow the Merced NWR driving tour past managed wetlands and pastures with Ross', snow, and cackling Canada geese, mallards, northern shovelers, and gadwalls. Up to 15,000 lesser sandhill cranes roost and feed in fields along with shorebirds, including rare mountain and snowy plovers.

Viewing Information: More than 200 bird species. High probability of seeing shorebirds, waterfowl, cranes, and white-faced ibis from fall to spring. Tundra swans are seen from January to February. Songbirds appear in spring. Wading birds and birds of prey are abundant year-round. Northern harriers and Swainson's hawks nest from March to May. Many small mammals, reptiles, amphibians. Call for information on viewing, visitor centers, tours, campground locations, handicap access. Allow a full day to drive all three loops. *PLEASE REMAIN ON DRIVING LOOPS; RESPECT PRIVATE PROPERTY SIGNS.*

Ownership: DFG, (209) 826-0463; DPR; USFWS, (209) 826-3508; private
Size: 116,660 acres **Closest Town:** Los Banos

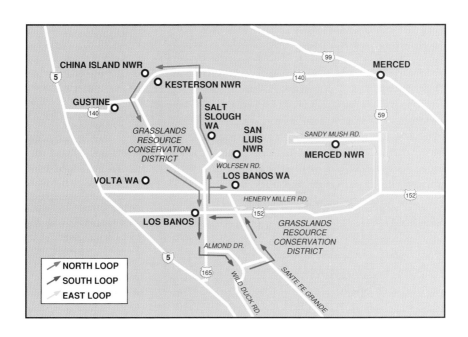

Ross' geese are common in California from fall through spring. Huge flocks, intermixed with other geese, can be seen resting on wetland ponds or feeding in nearby cultivated fields. They are smaller than their snow goose cousins and can be distinguished by their stubby pink bills and short necks.
GARY KRAMER

61 SAN LUIS DAM AND RESERVOIR

Description: Oak-studded foothills and steep, hidden canyons surround this large reservoir and forebays. Open water and coves draw wintering bald eagles, ruddy ducks, common goldeneyes, and western grebes; binoculars may provide views of up to 100,000 ducks on the lake. Abundant shorebirds join great blue herons and snowy egrets along the marshy shore. Golden eagles and red-tailed hawks scour the upper foothills, an area that sustains meadowlarks, horned larks, gopher snakes, and endangered San Joaquin Valley kit foxes. Look for black-tailed deer at Lower Cottonwood or other grassy hillsides.

Viewing Information: Birds of prey and deer are seen year-round. Watch for wading birds fall through spring. High probability of seeing waterfowl, shorebirds, and songbirds are abundant in winter. Easy car viewing. Several viewing areas at site. Managed by DPR.

Directions: From Interstate 5, drive west on Highway 152 about ten miles to reservoir and forebays.

Ownership: DWR, (209) 826-1196; USBR
Size: 24,000 acres **Closest Town:** Santa Nella

62 JOE DOMECQ WILDLIFE AREA

Description: Many layers of habitat begin at the Tuolumne River and rise steeply to an arid grassland with oaks and eucalyptus trees. Brush rabbits and valley quail inhabit the uplands, luring turkey vultures, red-tailed hawks, and golden eagles. Black-tailed deer feed in the open at dawn and dusk. Resident northern flickers, great horned owls, and yellow-billed magpies share the riparian forest with migratory western bluebirds, common yellowthroats, and American goldfinches. A beaver pond offers good views of muskrats and herons; watch for beavers in the evening. In the fall, view spawning chinook (king) salmon and bald eagles from the River Trail or Old Basso Bridge.

Viewing Information: Wading birds, beavers, and muskrats are seen year-round. Watch for birds of prey in fall, waterfowl in winter and spring. Songbirds are common in spring.

Directions: From Modesto on Highway 99, take Highway 132 east about thirty miles. Turn right on Lake Road, travel .25 mile and turn right at Old Basso Bridge fishing access.

Ownership: Stanislaus County (209) 525-4107
Size: 350 acres **Closest Town:** La Grange

Description: This is a rafter's paradise, where sixteen access points along fifty-nine miles of the meandering Stanislaus River between Goodwin Dam and the San Joaquin River offer outstanding river views of belted kingfishers, wood ducks, river otters, beavers, and many migratory ducks. Cliffs, canyons, massive oaks, and tangled grapes and blackberries border the river. Small mammals, band-tailed pigeons, and valley quail feast on acorns, surveyed by sharp-shinned hawks and American kestrels. During fall, stop at the Knight's Ferry Bridge to see spawning salmon. Spring wildflowers appear with migrant songbirds, including warblers, finches, hummingbirds, and sparrows.

Viewing Information: More than 225 bird species in area. High probability of seeing songbirds and waterfowl in spring. Wading birds, birds of prey, river otters, and beaver can be seen year-round. Visitor center at Knight's Ferry has access map. Campgrounds reached by boat only. *PLEASE DO NOT TRESPASS ON ADJACENT PRIVATE LANDS.*

Directions: *North of Modesto on Highway 99, take Highway 108 east about thirty miles to the Knight's Ferry Visitor Center.*

Ownership: ACE (209) 881-3517
Size: 625 acres **Closest Town:** Knight's Ferry

North America's smallest falcon, the American kestrel may often be viewed resting on a perch, or "hovering" over a field, searching for insects or mice. This colorful kestrel is a tercel, or male; females are less brilliantly colored.

JOHN HENDRICKSON

Birds rely on many cues to guide their migrations. Studies show that they orient themselves and navigate using land forms, wind direction, the sun, stars, the earth's magnetic fields, and even odors.

64 CASWELL MEMORIAL STATE PARK

Description: Virgin stands of massive valley oaks, trees native only to California, line a meandering stretch of the Stanislaus River lush with wild grapes and blackberries. The Oak Forest Nature Trail skirts the river and passes among trees more than 100 feet tall. Nuttall's woodpeckers, great horned owls, and wood ducks nest in well-used cavities. Resident scrub jays and valley quail are joined by spring-arriving Townsend's and MacGillivray's warblers, warbling vireos, and western tanagers. Black-headed grosbeaks, ash-throated flycatchers, and California thrashers nest in the area, as do Swainson's hawks. Fallen trees provide dens for opossums, skunks, raccoons, and a riparian brush rabbit found only at this park. Look for great blue herons, muskrats, and beavers at inland ponds or along the river. In the winter, watch overhead for waterfowl and listen for the low, hollow yodeling of sandhill cranes.

Viewing Information: More than 225 bird species at or near site. Watch for waterfowl in fall and winter. Songbirds, birds of prey, aquatic and small mammals, and some predators can be seen year-round. Salmon spawn in river at nearby sites.

Directions: *South of Manteca on Highway 99, take Austin Road exit west five miles to park.*

Ownership: DPR (209) 599-3810
Size: 258 acres   **Closest Town:** Ripon

Many a child feigning sleep has been accused of "playing possum," a saying derived from the opossum's habit of rolling over and closing its eyes when threatened. North America's only marsupial, the female opossum has a pouch where she nurses and carries up to fourteen youngsters.

MICHAEL SEWELL

Description: California's largest stand of valley oak riparian forest borders the largest undammed river. A trail passes a young, restored riparian forest, then moves to reconstructed marshes that attract wintering tundra swans, greater sandhill cranes, and scores of ducks. Long-billed curlews and other shorebirds forage in pastures and wetlands. River otters, beavers, and muskrats swim in cattail-lined sloughs, passing green herons and wood ducks. Riverside willows, blackberries, and wild grapes give way to an oak-studded savannah, areas favored by black-tailed deer, Nuttall's woodpeckers, and western bluebirds. The tallest trees bear the spring nests of Swainson's hawks.

Viewing Information: More than 200 birds species. Waterfowl, cranes, wading birds, and shorebirds are seen from October to March; birds of prey from November to April. Songbirds are common in fall and spring. Small boat access to Lost Slough from Delta Meadows Park. Bring mosquito repellent.

Directions: From Sacramento, take Interstate 5 south to Twin Cities Road exit. Drive east one mile to Franklin Road. Travel south on Franklin Road 1.5 miles to the Willow Slough trailhead, on left.

Ownership: Ducks Unlimited, (916) 684-2816;
TNC, (916) 363-8285; BLM; DFG
Size: 3,000   **Closest Town:** Galt

During migration, greater sandhill cranes fly in undulating wedges, filling the sky with their rattling, guttural calls. At night, they roost while standing in shallow water; by day, they disperse to nearby fields to feed. They are designated threatened in California because of loss of habitat and poor survival of their young. WILLIAM R. RADKE

66 EFFIE YEAW NATURE CENTER/ AMERICAN RIVER PARKWAY

Description: Cliff bluffs, forests, meadows, ponds, and a creek border this urban wildlife haven along the American River. Loop trails wind through the old river floodplain, where huge oaks, walnuts, elderberries, and wild grapes form a lush environment for acorn woodpeckers, sapsuckers, towhees, and other songbirds. Heavy understory offers cover for raccoons, skunks, and small mammals; Dutchman's pipevine attracts colorful pipevine swallowtail butterflies. Three small ponds provide water for California quail, turkeys, and black-tailed deer; tracks on pond and river banks may belong to bobcats, coyotes, river otters, or beavers. Herons wade along the shallow river edges and salmon spawn on the exposed river cobbles. Common mergansers, common goldeneyes, and wood ducks visit seasonally. Several birds of prey are residents.

Viewing Information: Watch for wood ducks, songbirds, and birds of prey in spring. Waterfowl, herons, turkeys, deer, and small mammals are seen year-round. Look for butterflies in early summer. Salmon spawn from November to December. Visitor center. Located on American River Parkway, a twenty-six-mile bike trail between Folsom Lake and downtown Sacramento.

Directions: *From Sacramento, take Highway 80 east (toward Reno) and take Madison Avenue East exit. Stay on Madison for almost nineteen miles and turn right on Manzanita. Travel 3.5 miles on Manzanita (name changes to Fair Oaks Boulevard). Turn left on Van Alstine and drive .4 mile; follow signs to nature center (located in Ancil Hoffman County Park).*

Ownership: Sacramento County (916) 489-4918
Closest Town: Carmichael

Adult salmon leave the ocean and swim up the Sacramento River, sometimes swimming hundreds of miles to spawn. Some salmon lay eggs in natural spawning riffles, such as those near Effie Yeaw Nature Center. Most climb the fish ladder below Nimbus Dam and are spawned at the fish hatchery.

DAVID BOZSIK

Description: Chinook salmon and steelhead migrating upriver cannot bypass Nimbus or Folsom dams to reach 120 miles of upstream spawning gravels. Some spawn on the seven-mile stretch between Watt Avenue and the dams; most use the fish ladder below Lake Natoma and spawn at Nimbus Hatchery, which raises four million salmon and 430,000 steelhead each year. Adjacent American River Hatchery raises several strains of rainbow trout.

Viewing Information: See salmon spawning and rearing in fall and early winter; steelhead in winter. Rainbow trout rearing can be seen year-round. Self-guiding tour. On American River Parkway. Handicap-accessible viewing.

Directions: From Sacramento, take Highway 50 to Hazel Avenue. Turn left, cross over freeway, and turn left at Nimbus Drive (first light). Immediately, turn right into hatcheries.

Ownership: DFG, (916) 355-0666; USBR (916) 355-0896
Size: Eleven acres   **Closest Town:** Rancho Cordova

68 ■ **FOLSOM LAKE STATE RECREATION AREA**

Description: This vast foothill lake, created by Folsom Dam, has seventy-five miles of shoreline and arms that extend up the north and south forks of the American River. Toyons, California buckeyes, and oaks shelter resident turkeys, black-tailed deer, and coyotes. Resident wrens, scrub jays, and California quail are joined by many migratory songbirds. Beavers and muskrats live at Mormon Island, a wetland that attracts Canada geese, white pelicans, and western grebes. Great blue herons nest among trees on Anderson Island. The American River Parkway bike and equestrian trail follows the river from Folsom Lake to Discovery Park in downtown Sacramento.

Viewing Information: High probability of seeing waterfowl fall, winter, and spring; songbirds in fall and spring. Explore the area by bicycle, boat, on horseback, or on eighty miles of trails.

Directions: From Sacramento, take Highway 50 east to Hazel Avenue. Turn left on Hazel, cross over freeway, and continue to Madison Avenue and turn right. Continue to Folsom-Auburn Road and turn left. Drive about three miles to Dam Road. Turn right and drive to park headquarters.

Ownership: DPR, (916) 988-0205; USBR
Size: 17,780 acres   **Closest Town:** Folsom

Description: A spectacular wetland within view of the Sutter Buttes. Wintering greater sandhill cranes share 6,600 acres of ponds with a million ducks and more than 80,000 Ross' and snow geese. American avocets, western sandpipers, and other shorebirds are common. Cattail-lined sloughs shelter pied-billed grebes, white-faced ibis, and black-crowned night herons; the heron rookery is visible from a viewing mound. Ring-necked pheasants are seen here, also tricolored blackbirds and other songbirds. River otters and muskrats appear occasionally. Barn owls, red-shouldered hawks, and black-shouldered kites patrol cultivated fields–a place to spot black-tailed deer some of which are albino.

Viewing Information: More than 230 bird species, with a Christmas bird count of more than 125 species. High probability of seeing waterfowl, sandhill cranes, and shorebirds in fall and winter; some species nest here. Songbirds and wading birds are seen fall through spring. Look for birds of prey year-round. Self-guiding trails. Tours. Excellent car viewing.

Directions: From junction of Interstate 5 and Highway 99, take Highway 99 north to Live Oak. Turn west on Pennington (North Butte) Road. Turn right on Almond Orchard Avenue and continue to entrance. Distance from Live Oak about eight miles.

Ownership: DFG (916) 846-5176
Size: 8,400 acres   **Closest Town:** Gridley

Sunset bathes this marsh at Gray Lodge Wildlife Area in rich hues of amber and gold. The sounds of calling ducks and geese fill the air as they return to ponds from fields where they have been feeding. It is a time of great drama, a time of tranquility. RON SANFORD

Description: The Sacramento Valley is the most important wintering site for waterfowl using the Pacific Flyway, attracting more than 1.5 million ducks and 750,000 geese. Surrounded by farmlands and flanked by the Sierra Nevada and Coast Range, the permanent ponds and seasonal marshes of the Sacramento National Wildlife Refuges are a wetland wildlife oasis. These man-made marshes, flooded in fall and winter, mimic seasonal cycles and are among the nation's most intensively managed refuges. Thousands of northern pintails and snow geese gather on ponds, joined by tundra swans, mallards, grebes, herons, and long-billed dowitchers. Migratory shorebirds and resident mammals attract more than a dozen species of birds of prey, including peregrine falcons. At least 100 songbird species have been observed here, including warblers, finches, swallows, and three types of blackbirds. The refuges offer good year-round views of many mammal species, ranging from black-tailed deer and jackrabbits to raccoons and muskrats.

Viewing Information: More than 265 bird species; many nesting. Waterfowl and birds of prey are common from November through January. Shorebirds, songbirds, herons, grebes, and white pelicans are seen year-round, best viewed in spring and fall. Driving tours at Sacramento and Colusa. Visitor center and viewing platform at Sacramento NWR.

Directions: See map. Sacramento NWR is six miles south of Willows.

Ownership: USFWS (916) 934-2801
Size: 23,047 acres   **Closest Town:** Willows

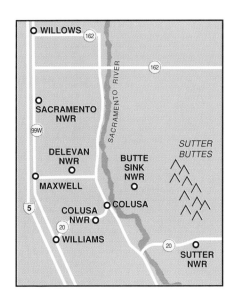

Description: Several forks of Stoney Creek flow from the Coast Range to this lake set among rolling oak woodlands, jagged lava flows, and the rock spires of the Black Buttes. Western fence lizards sun themselves on rocks that may hide Pacific rattlesnakes. The Buckhorn Trail winds among blue and valley oaks and offers views of mourning doves, Lewis' woodpeckers, black-tailed deer, and red-tailed hawks. The trail overlooks the lake, where western grebes, white pelicans, and other waterfowl cluster on the open water or in coves along the seven-mile shoreline. The Big Oak Trail meanders between Stoney Creek and Grizzly Flats, where lush vegetation attracts warblers, turkeys, and nesting great egrets and great blue herons. Brushy dams are evidence of beavers.

Viewing Information: Waterfowl, wading birds, birds of prey, songbirds, deer, beavers are seen in winter and spring; some are residents. Look for ospreys and bald eagles in winter, near water. Reptiles and small mammals are active year-round.

Directions: From Interstate 5, take Highway 32 exit and turn west on Newville Road (Road 200). Drive 9.5 miles to ACE headquarters and Observation Point.

Ownership: ACE (916) 865-4781
Size: 8,918 acres   **Closest Town:** Orland

From fields and woodlands to forests and deserts, the red-tailed hawk is at home anywhere in California. It feeds from an elevated perch in open areas and vigorously defends its nesting territory.

WILLIAM R. RADKE

72 LAKE RED BLUFF/SALMON VIEWING PLAZA

Description: This lake is a wide sweep of the Sacramento River backed up behind the Red Bluff Diversion Dam. Bank swallows nest along river banks; meadowlarks, warblers, and sparrows are abundant. Marshes shelter wood ducks, great blue herons, and occasional beavers. Turkeys often forage near the lake. Chinook salmon and steelhead attract ospreys and bald eagles. A salmon viewing plaza with underwater TV monitors overlooks two fish ladders and a fish research station.

Viewing Information: Songbird viewing is excellent in spring and summer. Waterfowl are abundant in fall and winter. Look for ospreys in spring and summer and bald eagles in winter. USFWS operates viewing plaza. Peak viewing of salmon, steelhead, shad, and squawfish is in August through October.

Directions: At Red Bluff on Interstate 5, turn east on Highway 36 (Antelope Road). Drive .2 mile to Sale Lane and turn right. Drive about one mile to lake; continue driving 1.4 miles to Salmon Viewing Plaza.

Ownership: USBR, (916) 824-5196; USFS, (916) 527-3043
Size: 489 acres   **Closest Town:** Red Bluff

73 BATTLE CREEK WILDLIFE AREA

Description: Battle Creek's natural spawning gravels for chinook salmon and adjacent Colman National Fish Hatchery are great places to watch fishing ospreys and bald eagles. Look for warblers, sparrows, wood ducks, belted kingfishers, raccoons, and gray foxes along the creek. Resident great blue herons, common egrets, and green herons are common. Bordering meadows and oaks attract black-tailed deer, turkeys, and hawks.

Viewing Information: Waterfowl are seen in fall and winter, ospreys and songbirds in spring and summer and bald eagles in winter. Battle Creek spawning is in fall. Hatchery spawning runs from September to November, with rearing of fish December through April. Restrooms, handicap access at hatchery.

Directions: From Interstate 5 southbound at Anderson, take Deschutes Road exit, drive east for 2.3 miles to Balls Ferry Road, and turn right. Drive three miles to Ash Creek Road and turn left. Travel 1.2 miles, then turn right on Gover Road. Drive 1.6 miles and turn left on Coleman Fish Hatchery Road. Wildlife area is before hatchery. Or from Interstate 5 northbound from Red Bluff, take Jellys Ferry Road east 14.2 miles to Coleman Fish Hatchery Road and turn right.

Ownership: DFG, (916) 225-2300; USFWS, (916) 365-8622
Size: 322 acres   **Closest Town:** Cottonwood

77

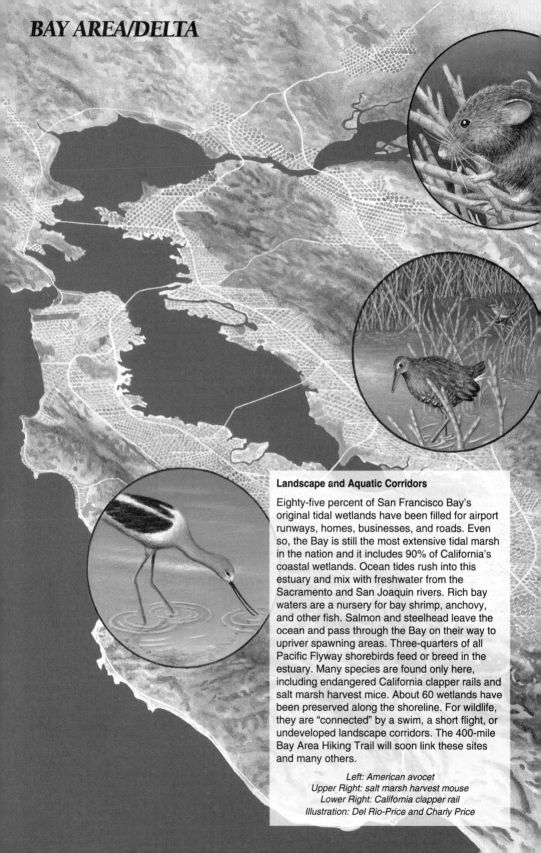

Landscape and Aquatic Corridors

Eighty-five percent of San Francisco Bay's original tidal wetlands have been filled for airport runways, homes, businesses, and roads. Even so, the Bay is still the most extensive tidal marsh in the nation and it includes 90% of California's coastal wetlands. Ocean tides rush into this estuary and mix with freshwater from the Sacramento and San Joaquin rivers. Rich bay waters are a nursery for bay shrimp, anchovy, and other fish. Salmon and steelhead leave the ocean and pass through the Bay on their way to upriver spawning areas. Three-quarters of all Pacific Flyway shorebirds feed or breed in the estuary. Many species are found only here, including endangered California clapper rails and salt marsh harvest mice. About 60 wetlands have been preserved along the shoreline. For wildlife, they are "connected" by a swim, a short flight, or undeveloped landscape corridors. The 400-mile Bay Area Hiking Trail will soon link these sites and many others.

Left: American avocet
Upper Right: salt marsh harvest mouse
Lower Right: California clapper rail
Illustration: Del Rio-Price and Charly Price

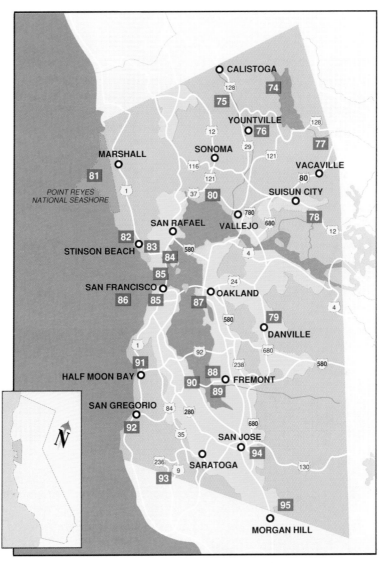

74 Lake Berryessa
75 Bothe-Napa Valley State Park
76 Napa River Ecological Reserve
77 Lake Solano Park
78 Grizzly Island Complex
79 Mount Diablo State Park
80 San Pablo Bay National
   Wildlife Refuge
81 Point Reyes
   National Seashore
82 Audubon Canyon Ranch/
   Bolinas Lagoon Preserve
83 Mount Tamalpais State Park
84 Richardson Bay
   Audubon Sanctuary

85 Golden Gate National
   Recreation Area
86 Farallon National Wildlife Refuge
87 Robert Crown Memorial
   State Beach
88 Coyote Hills Regional Park
89 San Francisco Bay National
   Wildlife Refuge
90 Palo Alto Baylands Preserve
91 Fitzgerald Marine Reserve
92 Pescadero Marsh
   Natural Preserve
93 Big Basin Redwoods State Park
94 Joseph D. Grant County Park
95 Henry Coe State Park

74 LAKE BERRYESSA

Description: Grassy hills dotted with oaks, ceanothus, and manzanita surround long inlets and coves populated by migratory tundra swans, Canada geese, mallards, ruddy ducks, and cinnamon teal. White pelicans, western grebes, and buffleheads fish the open water along with California gulls, ospreys, and bald eagles. Watch for black phoebes, green herons, and lesser sandhill cranes near the shoreline or along the Smittle Creek Trail. Nearly twenty species of birds of prey have been sighted, including resident turkey vultures, Cooper's hawks, American kestrels, and barn owls. Coveys of California quail feed in the grasslands just after sunrise and before sunset. The oaks and chaparral attract many birds, including Bewick's wrens, Audubon's warblers, western bluebirds, and northern flickers.

Viewing Information: High probability of seeing waterfowl, songbirds, shorebirds, and wading birds from October through April. Birds of prey are seen year-round; bald and golden eagles are present from November through February. Look for deer and small mammals year-round. Wildflowers bloom from February to April.

Directions: *Take Highway 128 north of Napa Valley about ten miles to Knoxville Road; turn and drive ten miles to lake.*

Ownership: USBR (707) 966-2111
Size: 5,700 acres   **Closest Town:** Napa

Acorn woodpeckers are known for their uncommon food storage methods. Holes are pre-drilled in oaks, nearby pines, even utility poles, and acorns are jammed securely into the openings, ready for "harvest" when food supplies are scarce. An entire family of acorn woodpeckers may use the same tree or pole.

JEFF FOOTT

BOTHE-NAPA VALLEY STATE PARK

Description: This rugged Napa Valley canyon is highlighted by volcanic ash cliffs and a streamside redwood forest. The Redwood Trail follows Ritchey Creek through second-growth redwoods and spring-blooming orchids; listen here for noisy Steller's jays. Resident woodpeckers here include northern flickers and hairy, downy, Nutall's, acorn, and pileated woodpeckers. North-facing slopes shelter spotted owls, ravens, and ruby-crowned kinglets. The Coyote Peak Trail passes through chaparral woodlands favored by California quail, scrub jays, and black-tailed deer.

Viewing Information: Look for woodpeckers from March through October. Songbirds are common in spring. Spotted owls may be seen from March through August. Visitor center. Viewing mostly by trail or on horseback.

Directions: *From Calistoga, take Highway 29/128 south four miles to Larkmead Lane and park entrance. Park at trailhead sign.*

Ownership: DPR (707) 942-5370
Size: 1,900 acres   **Closest Town:** Calistoga

NAPA RIVER ECOLOGICAL RESERVE

Description: Massive valley oaks and California bays shade the Napa River and Conn Creeks, one of the Bay Area's best examples of an old-growth riparian woodland. While raccoons, skunks, squirrels, opossums, and even minks reside here, birds are the prime attraction. Tree cavities attract red-breasted sapsuckers, acorn and downy woodpeckers, tree and violet-green swallows, and screech, barn, and great horned owls. The forest canopy and dense understory shelter many migrant songbirds and breeding yellow warblers, Anna's hummingbirds, even yellow-breasted chats. Spring butterflies and wildflowers are abundant.

Viewing Information: More than 200 bird species; many nesting. Cavity nesters are abundant from March through June, common in fall and winter. Songbirds are seen year-round, best viewing is in spring. An undeveloped site. *IN FLOODPLAIN; WET IN WINTER. LOTS OF POISON OAK.*

Directions: *North of Yountville on Highway 29, turn east on Oakville Cross Road. Drive 2.5 miles and turn right on Silverado Trail. Drive 2.3 miles to Yountville Cross Road, turn right, and drive .9 miles to reserve parking area.*

Ownership: DFG (707) 944-5500
Size: Seventy-three acres   **Closest Town:** Yountville

77 LAKE SOLANO PARK

Description: Putah Creek flows from Lake Berryessa into narrow Lake Solano, then meanders through Davis and flows into the Yolo Bypass. Creekside vegetation hums with the summer songs of western blue birds, meadowlarks, and cedar waxwings. The lake, rocky outcroppings, riparian vegetation, and oak woodlands are home to more than a dozen resident mammals, including beavers, minks, raccoons, and black-tailed deer. Quiet lake waters lure wintering trumpeter swans, wood ducks, and European wigeons; a half-dozen fish species draw buffleheads, western grebes, and lesser scaups. Other winter visitors include great blue herons, common snipes, bandtail pigeons, and ospreys. The grassy uplands offer excellent winter views of feral pigs, American kestrels, turkeys, and valley quail.

Viewing Information: Best viewing early morning, late afternoon. Look for waterfowl from November to February. Songbirds are seen year-round; migrants stay from May to October. Birds of prey, deer, and small mammals are active year-round; look for beavers in spring. Good views from DFG fishing accesses on Putah Creek/Park.

Directions: West of Vacaville on Highway 80, take the Pe:a Adobe Road exit north to Pleasant Valley Road. Drive about thirteen miles to lake.

Ownership: Solano County (916) 795-2990
Size: 110 acres   **Closest Town:** Winters

Creekside blackberries and wild grapes offer good views of feeding ceder waxwings, named for the red waxy substances found on the adult birds' feather shafts. These colorful birds often forage in large groups, occasionally passing berries from bird to bird.

SALLY MYERS

Description: Grizzly Island is located in the Suisun Marsh, the largest continuous estuarine marsh in the lower forty-eight states. Salt marshes, tidal flats, seasonal ponds, and uplands shelter 250,000 wintering waterfowl, thousands of shorebirds, dozens of songbird species, and seven protected species, including endangered salt marsh harvest mice. This is one of three significant wintering areas in the world for tule geese. California's largest population of river otters swim the abundant sloughs. Riparian vegetation hides several heron species, clapper rails, and elusive black rails. Some species, such as the Suisun aster, shrew, and suisun sparrow, are found nowhere else on earth. Managed ponds host cinnamon teal, northern pintails, and white pelicans; some remain to breed. Songbirds include marsh wrens, common yellowthroats, and many others. Northern harriers, short-eared owls, golden eagles, and other birds of prey hunt upland fields that also sustain tule elk, a species native only to California.

Viewing Information: More than 230 bird species. Peak viewing month is February. High probability of seeing wading birds year-round. Birds of prey are seen year-round, particularly in fall and winter. Waterfowl and shorebirds are common in winter, with many summer broods. Look for songbirds in winter and small and aquatic mammals year-round. Watch tule elk rut in fall and see calves in spring. Excellent car viewing. Seventy-five miles of levee trails open February through July. See marsh restoration projects.

Directions: *At Fairfield and Highway 80, take Highway 12 east about four miles. Turn south on Grizzly Island Road. Drive nine miles to DGF headquaters.*

Ownership: DFG (707) 425-3828
Size: 14,300 acres   **Closest Town:** Suisun City

Grizzly Island lies in the heart of the Suisun Marsh, the largest contiguous brackish marsh in the continental United States. A variety of wading birds find good fishing in the meandering sloughs, also good places to look for river otters and elusive salt marsh harvest mice.

FRANK S. BALTHIS

79 MOUNT DIABLO STATE PARK

Description: Rolling savannahs with a mosaic of oaks and chaparral surround this famous Bay Area peak, with unobstructed views of more land area than anywhere else in the world except Mount Kilimanjaro. Abundant rodents and small mammals draw red-tailed hawks, American kestrels, and golden eagles by day; the night hunt is left to great horned, barn, and screech owls. Brushy chaparral hides blue-gray gnatcatchers, horned larks, and brush rabbits, while open areas sustain more than a dozen species of snakes, including western rattlesnakes. High on the mountain slopes, western tanagers, cedar waxwings, warblers, and swallows perch among the oaks and digger pines. Turkey vultures roost near the peak. Black-tailed deer, raccoons, and western gray squirrels are common; foxes, bobcats, coyotes, and even mountain lions have been spotted from park trails.

Viewing Information: Songbirds are common in spring and summer. Birds of prey, small mammals, and deer are seen year-round. Spring is best for wildflowers. About 150 miles of trails. Summit overlook and visitor center.

Directions: *From Highway 680 at Danville, take Diablo Road 1.5 miles. Bear right onto Mt. Diablo Scenic Blvd., then continue 2.5 miles to park entrance.*

Ownership: DPR (510) 837-2525
Size: 20,090 acres   **Closest Town:** Danville

Green in the winter and golden in the summer, Mt. Diablo's rolling oak-studded hills shelter everything from mountain lions and bobcats to western tanagers and cedar waxwings. This Bay Area landmark offers exceptional, 360 degree views, encompassing more than 40,000 square miles. MICHAEL SEWELL

Description: This salt marsh and upland fields are just a few miles from a major Bay Area freeway, but the area feels isolated and the only city in sight is San Francisco, across the bay. The three-mile hike to the wetland follows a road closed to vehicles bordered by Tolay Creek and grassy fields. Northern harriers and black-shouldered kites cross the skies above, while herons and egrets fish along the creek. Riparian vegetation shelters fox sparrows and meadowlarks. The road ends at Tubbs Island, where a hiking loop explores the bay and salt marsh, with views of white pelicans, canvasbacks, and scaups. Look here for long-legged shorebirds such as willets and godwits. Harbor seals haul out along the shore. Follow a second hiking loop inland to marshes and ponds favored by dabbling ducks, sandpipers, and black-necked stilts.

Viewing Information: More than 200 bird species; many residents. High probability of seeing waterfowl and shorebirds from October to April. Wading birds, songbirds, and birds of prey are seen year-round. An undeveloped site; limited parking. Walk-in viewing only. On San Francisco Bay Trail.

Directions: *From Marin or East Bay, take Highway 37 .25 mile east of the junction of highways 37 and 121. Entrance on south side of highway.*

Ownership: USFWS (510) 792-0222
Size: 13,500 acres   **Closest Town:** Vallejo

Most canvasbacks using the Pacific Flyway stopover in San Francisco Bay. The male is sometimes confused with a redhead, which has a golden eye and a blue bill. Canvasbacks fly in small wedges and can be recognized aloft by their rapid wingbeats, which create a flickering of white as they fly. TOM & PAT LEESON

81 POINT REYES NATIONAL SEASHORE

Description: One of the best birding areas in the western United States, with forty-five percent of North America's bird species. Fir and pine forests border bay, maple, and oak woodlands. Meadows, streams, lakes, and lagoons lie near a coastline dotted with beaches, dunes, and tidepools. Two major estuaries attract scores of shorebirds and waterfowl, including sanderlings, greater yellowlegs, northern pintails, and American and Eurasian wigeons. Coastal trees camouflage migratory birds; some, such as western flycatchers and Anna's hummingbirds, breed here. Tomales Point sustains resident tule elk; black-tailed deer are everywhere. Harbor seals, sea lions, and gray whales pass close to Point Reyes Lighthouse, also a summer nesting site for common murres. At dusk, watch myotis bats flying from the red barn near the entrance.

Viewing Information: 430 bird species. Wading birds and gulls are seen year-round. Look for songbirds in fall, with some eastern migrants. Shorebirds are common in fall and winter and waterfowl stay from November through April. Look for nesting osprey and red-shouldered hawks. Raccoons, skunks, gray foxes, and brush rabbits are active year-round. Bats can be seen from March to May. More than 850 flowering plants. Visitor centers at Bear Valley, Drakes Beach, and Lighthouse. Camping by permit only. *BEWARE OF LOOSE ROCK AND STEEP CLIFFS.*

Directions: *Take Highway 1 to Olema. Turn west on Bear Valley Road and follow signs to park headquarters or to Bear Valley Visitor Center.*

Ownership: NPS (415) 663-1092
Size: 71,049 acres   **Closest Town:** Point Reyes Station

Easily identified by its spots and short, "bobbed" tail, North America's most common wild feline is the bobcat. It normally hunts at night, guided by superb vision, but daytime sightings are not unusual. Like other cats, the bobcat's whiskers are extremely sensitive, helping to guide it through narrow places.

MICHAEL SEWELL

Description: This sanctuary encompasses Bolinas Ridge's forested slopes, redwood groves, and a salt marsh estuary. A trail bordered by live oaks, California laurels, and spring wildflowers leads to wooden benches and spotting scopes that overlook a common egret and great blue heron rookery. In January, egrets and herons perform dramatic courtship dances and displays. Their nests are arranged in tiers in the trees; as many as 175 nests may be seen. Nestlings appear in late spring and fledging is complete by summer's end. Watch egrets and herons feed in Bolinas Lagoon, which sustains twenty-five fish species that also attract ospreys, gulls, and diving ducks. Look for more waterfowl and shorebirds in the shallow channels. The forest, grasslands, and ponds host black-tailed deer, songbirds, birds of prey, and several small mammals.

Viewing Information: Rookery viewing is excellent April through June. Birds of prey and deer are seen year-round. Waterfowl and marine birds in fall and spring. Visitor center. Several pullouts on Highway 1 to view lagoon.

Directions: *From Stinson Beach, take Highway 1 north three miles to entrance.*

Ownership: Marin, Golden Gate, and Sequoia Audubon Societies (415) 868-9244
Size: 1,000 acres   **Closest Town:** Stinson Beach

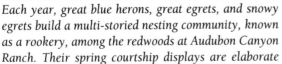

Each year, great blue herons, great egrets, and snowy egrets build a multi-storied nesting community, known as a rookery, among the redwoods at Audubon Canyon Ranch. Their spring courtship displays are elaborate rituals of crest raising, bill clacking, circling flights, and twig shaking. A viewing platform with spotting scopes affords excellent views of this wildlife spectacle.

FRANK S. BALTHIS PHOTOS

83 MOUNT TAMALPAIS STATE PARK

Description: Coastal terraces and deep canyons lined with redwoods and ferns give way to higher stands of fir, oak-studded grasslands, and chaparral, culminating at 2,571-foot Mount Tamalpais. On a clear day, there are spectacular views of San Francisco Bay, Mount Diablo, the Farallon Islands, even the Sierra Nevada. More than 200 miles of trails crisscross this near-urban wilderness and adjacent public lands. Grassy woodlands offer views of black-tailed deer, gray foxes, and an occasional bobcat. Ravens, Steller's jays, acorn woodpeckers, western bluebirds, California quail, and bats are common. Gray squirrels and other rodents attract sharp-shinned hawks, red-tailed hawks, and turkey vultures by day. Several owl species are active at night, along with raccoons, mountain lions, and seldom-seen ringtails, a wary, nocturnal mammal.

Viewing Information: *WINDING, HEAVILY-TRAVELED ROADS.* More than 150 bird species, many residents. Birds of prey, deer, and small mammals are seen year-round. Look for songbirds in spring. Visitor center. Some car viewing. Park surrounds Muir Woods National Monument and is bordered by Golden Gate NRA, Marin Municipal Water District.

Directions: *From Golden Gate Bridge, take Highway 101 north to Stinson Beach/ Highway 1 exit. Follow Highway 1 about two miles to Panoramic Highway; turn right. Continue five miles to park headquarters at Pantoll Camp.*

Ownership: DPR (415) 388-2070, (415) 456-1286
Size: 6,300 acres   **Closest Town:** Mill Valley

The California gray squirrel, with its erect, plume-like tail, belongs to a family whose scientific name means "shade-tail." They busily store nuts underground, finding them when food is scarce not from memory, but by their scent. Listen for the chattering and chirping of these vocal animals.

TOM & PAT LEESON

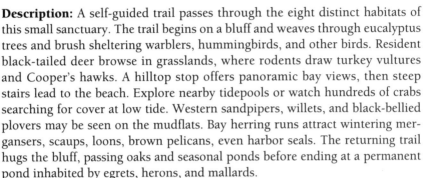

Description: A self-guided trail passes through the eight distinct habitats of this small sanctuary. The trail begins on a bluff and weaves through eucalyptus trees and brush sheltering warblers, hummingbirds, and other birds. Resident black-tailed deer browse in grasslands, where rodents draw turkey vultures and Cooper's hawks. A hilltop stop offers panoramic bay views, then steep stairs lead to the beach. Explore nearby tidepools or watch hundreds of crabs searching for cover at low tide. Western sandpipers, willets, and black-bellied plovers may be seen on the mudflats. Bay herring runs attract wintering mergansers, scaups, loons, brown pelicans, even harbor seals. The returning trail hugs the bluff, passing oaks and seasonal ponds before ending at a permanent pond inhabited by egrets, herons, and mallards.

Viewing Information: More than 200 bird species, many residents. Pelicans and terns are seen in fall and winter. Waterfowl are abundant in winter. Shorebird and songbird viewing is excellent in fall and spring at this Western Hemisphere Shorebird Reserve Network site. Occasional willow flycatchers, black-headed grosbeaks. Harbor seals can be seen in fall and winter. Visitor center. On San Francisco Bay Trail. *WATCH FOR POISON OAK.*

Directions: From Tiburon on Highway 101, take Tiburon Boulevard/Highway 13 exit west. Drive one mile and turn right on Greenwood Cove Drive. Continue .25 mile to entrance.

Ownership: National Audubon Society (415) 388-2524
Size: 911 acres   **Closest Town:** Tiburon

During breeding, snowy egrets are marked with a veil of fine feathers. In the 1800's, the plumes were so popular for womens' hats that the egrets were nearly decimated. Both parents take turns on the nest and the one sitting is very protective. Its mate must return to the nest with a special display or it could face an attack.

M.D. CONLIN

85 GOLDEN GATE NATIONAL RECREATION AREA

Description: A huge complex spanning three urban counties. Wildlife habitats range from cliff-lined beaches, estuaries, lagoons, and islands to undisturbed grasslands, forested ridges, and lush redwood groves. The San Francisco side includes Alcatraz, starts at Aquatic Park and follows the coast to Fort Funston and Ocean Beach. In the uplands, Sweeney Ridge harbors songbirds and butterflies. Boat tours visit Alcatraz, once a prison, now a shelter for nesting colonies of black-crowned night herons and western gulls. Shorebirds roam the San Francisco shorelines; western grebes, Brandt's cormorants, pigeon guillemots, and brown pelicans (endangered in the West) remain offshore. Seal Rocks below the Cliff House are a favorite haul out for Steller and California sea lions. The vast Marin side encompasses nearly all of the Marin Headlands, Tennessee Valley, three military bases, and separate lands at Muir Woods and Stinson Beach. Quiet Rodeo Lagoon and Beach attract a broad range of waterfowl, wading birds, and gulls, including breeding pelagic cormorants and wintering harlequin and tufted ducks. An extensive headland trail system explores varied habitats with songbirds, birds of prey, spring wildflowers, and spectacular bay and ocean vistas; watch for bobcats and gray foxes. Be sure to visit Hawk Hill at Battery 129 in the fall; nineteen raptor species—up to 12,000 birds—pass over this site, forming the largest concentration of migratory hawks in the Pacific states.

Viewing Information: Good year-round views of some waterfowl, wading birds, marine birds, shorebirds, birds of prey, songbirds, seals, sea lions, and small mammals. Waterfowl and shorebirds are best seen October to April. Hawk Hill viewing is excellent from August through December; September and October are peak months. Alcatraz boat tours, fee; sometimes reservation required. Visitor centers. On San Francisco Bay Trail.

Directions: *San Francisco side: Get park map at headquarters located at Fort Mason on Bay and Franklin Streets. Marin Headlands area: North of the Golden Gate Bridge, take first Sausalito exit and follow park signs to visitor center.*

Ownership: NPS (415) 556-0560
Size: 73,183 acres   **Closest Town:** San Francisco

 Shorebirds move in and out from shore with tides, feeding in and near the water's edge. Look closely at their specialized beaks and legs. Long legs, long beaks, and even long necks allowing feeding in deeper water or beneath mudflats.

Description: Seven wave-eroded outcroppings rise from the ocean thirty miles west of San Francisco. These islands are surrounded by such a productive marine environment that a portion has been designated a National Marine Sanctuary. Few ocean regions are as bountiful. As many as twelve sea bird species are found here, with nearly 300,000 birds annually. This is the largest continental seabird breeding colony south of Alaska. Rocky slopes and underground burrows shelter the world's largest breeding colonies of ashy storm petrels, Brandt's cormorants, and western gulls. Most of the state's Cassin's auklets nest here. The Farallons are also the northernmost breeding site for 7,000 seals and sea lions, including northern elephant seals and California and Steller sea lions. Gray whales and porpoises pass close to the islands.

Viewing Information: Islands closed to public. Boat tour information available from USFWS. Best time to view, November to March. *BOATS MUST REMAIN 300 FEET OFFSHORE.*

Ownership: USFWS (510) 792-0222
Size: 211 acres

The windswept, rocky slopes of the Farallon Islands support thousands of breeding seals, sea lions, and the world's largest breeding colonies of several sea birds, including Brandt's cormorants. The sky-blue throat pouch on these primitive-looking cormorants is more evident during breeding. JEFF FOOTT

87 ROBERT CROWN MEMORIAL STATE BEACH

Description: Alameda's protected bay shore shelters Crab Cove, California's first marine/estuarine reserve, and Elsie Roemer Bird Sanctuary, an adjacent saltwater marsh. Rocky shore, mudflats, and shallow tidal areas with sea lettuce, pickleweed, and cordgrass are rich with crabs, sea hares, and other marine life. Grebes, loons, and cormorants dive for fish in the deeper water. Look for American wigeons, Caspian's terns, and snowy egrets closer to shore or from boardwalks over marsh ponds. Marbled godwits, black-bellied plovers, and other shorebirds feed on the tidal flats. Gulls, terns, and killdeer prowl the sandy beaches. Marsh vegetation at the adjacent bird sanctuary hides sora and endangered clapper rails. Song sparrows, western meadowlarks, and other songbirds inhabit the drier uplands.

Viewing Information: About 150 bird species; many resident and nesting. Look for waterfowl from October through April. Shorebirds, songbirds, and wading birds are seen year-round. Hands-on visitor center open March to November. On San Francisco Bay Trail. *DO NOT COLLECT OR DISTURB MARINE OR PLANT LIFE.*

Directions: *From Highway 880 in Oakland, take Broadway Exit. Drive through Alameda Tube onto Webster Street. Continue about 1.5 miles to Central and turn right. Go one block to McKay Street and turn left. Entrance at end of street.*

Ownership: East Bay Regional Parks (510) 521-6887, (510) 531-9300
Size: 150 acres   **Closest Town:** Alameda

Eight-five percent of San Francisco Bay tidal wetlands have been lost to development, jeopardizing the survival of several species, including the secretive California clapper rail. This bird is now endangered and relegated to just a handful of bay marshes. Rails are easiest to spot dashing for cover during high tides. JEFF FOOTT

88 COYOTE HILLS REGIONAL PARK

Description: Cattail-rimmed marshes give way to grassy, oak-studded shoreline hills with panoramic views of South San Francisco Bay. Elevated boardwalks lead to tranquil ponds, where northern pintails, gadwalls, and California gulls rest and breed. Shorebirds such as snowy plovers and American avocets are year-round residents. Riparian vegetation lining ponds and Alameda Creek reveals raccoons and gray fox, but camouflages American bitterns and black-crowned night herons. A changing collection of warblers, swallows, flycatchers, and wrens supplies year-round birdsong. Grassy uplands attract black-tailed deer, great horned owls, northern harriers, and black-shouldered kites. Shoreline hills with bay vistas overlook flocks of scaups and grebes; the shoreline trail passes tidal flats with Forster's terns, snowy egrets, and shorebirds.

Viewing Information: More than 200 bird species, four endangered, many nesting. Waterfowl, shorebirds, wading birds, songbirds, birds of prey, and deer are seen year-round. Peak viewing of waterfowl and birds of prey in fall and winter. Some car viewing, many trails, visitor center. Connected to San Francisco Bay NWR by trail. On San Francisco Bay Trail.

Directions: *From junction of highways 880 and 84 in Fremont, take Highway 84 west. Drive about one mile to Paseo Padre Parkway exit and turn right. Drive .8 mile to Patterson Ranch Road and turn left. Drive one mile to entrance.*

Ownership: East Bay Regional Parks (510) 795-9385
Size: 1,064 acres　　**Closest Town:** Fremont

Known for its bushy striped tail and black mask, the raccoon is found near wooded streams throughout the state—though it is equally at home in urban backyards. Raccoons often wash their food, not to get it clean, but rather to feel for objects they shouldn't eat.

TOM & PAT LEESON

89 SAN FRANCISCO BAY NATIONAL WILDLIFE REFUGE

Description: Grassy uplands overlook salt ponds, salt marshes, mudflats, and meandering tidal channels at this south bay refuge. A nature trail winds through the uplands, where northern harriers and peregrine falcons look for prey. The path descends to salt ponds and mudflats teeming with western sandpipers, dunlins, and other shorebirds. Pickleweed and cordgrass line slough channels and ponds favored by willets, black-necked stilts, egrets, and herons; endangered salt marsh harvest mice and clapper rails hide among this vegetation. Thousands of ducks raft up in the open water, including concentrations of northern pintails, northern shovelers, and canvasbacks. Harbor seals may be seen near shore. Watch for terns hunting fish, including the least tern, an endangered species on the West Coast.

Viewing Information: More than 250 bird species. High probability of seeing shorebirds and waterfowl from October through April. Look for songbirds in spring and summer. Many resident birds, mammals, and reptiles. Connected to Coyote Hills by trail. On San Francisco Bay Trail.

Directions: From Highway 880 in Fremont, take Highway 84 west two miles to the Thornton Avenue exit. Drive over highway and turn right onto Marshlands Road. Continue to visitor center.

Ownership: USFWS (510) 792-0222
Size: 20,000 acres   **Closest Town:** Fremont

Like other bay wetland species, the endangered salt marsh harvest mouse has lost crucial habitat to development. This timid animal lives among pickleweed, building runways and nests within the dense cover, and even subsisting on saltwater. During high tides, watch for stranded mice clinging tenaciously to the swaying plants.

B. "MOOSE" PETERSON

90 PALO ALTO BAYLANDS PRESERVE

Description: These tranquil bay waters, salt marshes, and freshwater wetlands are just a mile from a major freeway. Offshore, California gulls, double-crested cormorants, western grebes, and resident harbor seals feed on bay shrimp, Pacific herring, and soft-shelled clams. Winter high tides may reveal salt marsh harvest mice clinging to pickleweed, or endangered clapper rails running for cover among the cordgrass. Northern shovelers and gadwalls feed in the estuary or at the preserve's pond. An adjacent flood-control basin attracts wading birds and ducks. Trees and brush shelter red-winged blackbirds, common yellowthroats, and other songbirds, many of which nest.

Viewing Information: More than 150 bird species. High likelihood of seeing waterfowl, shorebirds, and wading birds from fall to spring. Marine birds are seen in winter. Look for birds of prey year-round, particularly in winter. Trails, boardwalks, visitor center. On San Francisco Bay Trail.

Directions: From Palo Alto on Highway 101, take the Embarcadero Road East exit. Drive 1.5 miles to "T" junction, turn left, and continue to visitor center.

Ownership: City of Palo Alto (415) 329-2506
Size: 2,000 acres **Closest Town:** Palo Alto

91 FITZGERALD MARINE RESERVE

Description: Sandstone cliffs tower fifty feet above rocky shale reefs and sandy beaches that comprise one of California's most diverse intertidal regions. Tidepools exposed by low and medium tides reveal sea palms, surf grass, sea urchins, sea anemones, sea stars, nudibranches, and crabs. The area boasts scores of intertidal species, including nearly fifty at the northern or southern extent of their range. Offshore kelp beds hide rockfish, cabezon, and other fish. Shorebirds, waterfowl, and marine birds visit seasonally. Grassy uplands and Monterey cypress provide habitat for songbirds, birds of prey, and black-tailed deer.

Viewing Information: Consult tidetables. Limited parking. *NO COLLECTING. DO NOT DISTURB MARINE LIFE. ROCKS CAN BE SLIPPERY.* Shorebirds are best viewed in winter, waterfowl in fall and spring.

Directions: At Moss Beach on Highway 1, turn west on California Avenue. Drive to parking area.

Ownership: San Mateo County (415) 728-3584
Size: Thirty acres **Closest Town:** Moss Beach

Common at most wetlands, American avocets are social birds; hundreds may rest and feed together. A long line of avocets may at times fan out in the shallows, submerging their heads and sweeping their long upturned bills from side to side, probing for insects, seeds, and other edibles. MIKE DANZENBAKER

Description: Hills dotted with coyote brush give way to creeks, brackish ponds, sand dunes forty feet high, tidal flats, and a salt marsh that forms the largest wetland between San Francisco Bay and Elkhorn Slough. Sandpipers, plovers, dowitchers, and other shorebirds are seen on the sandy tidal flats east of the Highway 1 bridge. The marsh is home to western pond turtles, endangered San Francisco garter snakes, mallards, cinnamon teal, marsh wrens, common yellowthroats, and red-winged blackbirds. Egrets and herons wade in the marsh, roosting and nesting in nearby eucalyptus trees. Woodlands shelter downy woodpeckers, olive-sided flycatchers, and bats. Mice and rabbits hide in the scrub flats, attracting northern harriers and peregrine falcons. The estuary is a nursery for many species; steelhead, salmon, and other fish spawn in upstream waters.

Viewing Information: More than 250 bird species. Probability of seeing waterfowl and shorebirds is high in fall and spring, moderate in winter. Look for songbirds in spring. Wading birds and birds of prey are seen year-round. Good viewing along Pescadero Road pullouts and marsh trails. *WATCH FOR POISON OAK AND TICKS.*

Directions: *From Half Moon Bay, take Highway 1 fifteen miles south to state beach parking areas and walk to marsh.*

Ownership: DPR (415) 879-0832
Size: 588 acres   **Closest Town:** Pescadero

The once-common San Francisco garter snake is now endangered, residing at just a few dozen development-free sites in San Mateo and Santa Cruz counties, including Pescadero Marsh. Look for them near ponds and creeks, where they prey on frogs and fish. On warm, fall days, watch sunny hillsides for groups of snakes mating. FRANK S. BALTHIS

93 BIG BASIN REDWOODS STATE PARK

Description: California's oldest state park begins at forested ridges over 2,000 feet high, encompasses gorges with cascading waterfalls, and ends at a freshwater marsh bordered by dunes and sandy beach. Turkey vultures and red-tailed hawks favor the rocky slopes, where evergreens and chaparral support hummingbirds, warblers, and doves. Resident black-tailed deer, California gray squirrels and raccoons are abundant and easily seen. Massive redwood trees along Waddell Creek hide brown creepers, American dippers, marbled murrelets, and bats. The moist environment sustains California newts, Pacific giant salamanders, and Pacific tree frogs. The Skyline to the Sea Trail begins at nearby Castle Rock, passes through Big Basin uplands, and ends at the beach with views of gulls, terns, and harbor seals. Across Highway 1, Waddell Creek Marsh attracts herons, egrets, legions of shorebirds, and salmon or steelhead bound for the creek.

Viewing Information: Low to moderate probability of seeing wading birds and birds of prey year-round. Look for songbirds in winter and spring. Shorebirds and marine birds are common in winter. Watch for marbled murrelets from April through August leaving forest at sunrise. One hundred miles of trails. Visitor center.

Directions: From Saratoga or Santa Cruz, take Highway 9 to Highway 236. Follow Highway 236 nine miles to park. Beach and marsh entrance off of Highway 1, north of Santa Cruz.

Ownership: DPR (408) 338-6132
Size: 19,000 acres   **Closest Town:** Boulder Creek

Despite its name, the Pacific treefrog will be spotted along streams, rock crevices, and culverts more often than it will be seen in a tree. This brilliantly-colored frog with the conspicuous black eyestripe thrives at Big Basin and other areas where streams or ponds are available.

ERWIN & PEGGY BAUER

94 JOSEPH D. GRANT COUNTY PARK

Description: Great blue herons wade in the shallows of Grant Lake, the largest of four ponds at this urban woodland park. Wintering bald eagles fish among scaups, ring-necked ducks, and other divers; dabbling ducks forage in the the shallows. Bobcats and raccoons leave tracks on the shoreline, where vegetation hides brown towhees, red-winged blackbirds, and California quail. Wet meadows offer summer views of western meadowlarks, turkeys, and black-tailed deer. Black-shouldered kites, red-tailed hawks, golden eagles, and northern harriers are also common.

Viewing Information: Wading birds, songbirds, and birds of prey are seen year-round; high probability of seeing songbirds and birds of prey in spring. Look for waterfowl from September to mid-March. Visitor center.

Directions: *From Highway 680 or Highway 101, take Alum Rock Avenue east to Mount Hamilton Road and turn right. Drive eight miles to entrance.*

Ownership: Santa Clara County Parks (408) 274-6121
Size: 9,522 acres   **Closest Town:** San Jose

95 HENRY COE STATE PARK

Description: This rugged wilderness park's grassy woodlands and chaparral are broken by the canyons and ridges of the Diablo mountain range. Abundant grasslands attract black-tailed deer, western meadowlarks, and golden eagles. Brushy slopes are favored by California quail, mourning doves, scrub jays, brush rabbits, even mountain lions. China Hole, a pool in Coyote Creek, shelters western pond turtles, rough-skinned newts, and towhees. Acorn woodpeckers, feral pigs, and turkeys inhabit the oaks while Nuttall's woodpeckers and red-tailed hawks make ridge-top ponderosa pines their home. Year-round, watch for western rattlesnakes, and gopher and king snakes.

Viewing Information: Moderate probability of seeing most wildlife year-round. Songbirds are best seen in spring. 200 wildflower species. Visitor center. Wilderness park accessed by horse and foot trails only. *DUNNE ROAD IS WINDING AND STEEP; ALLOW HALF-HOUR FOR DRIVE. RUGGED HIKING TRAILS; CARRY DRINKING WATER.*

Directions: *At Morgan Hill on Highway 101, take East Dunne Avenue exit east thirteen miles to park.*

Ownership: DPR (408) 779-2728
Size: 68,000 acres   **Closest Town:** Morgan Hill

CENTRAL COAST

Waves, Wind, and Time

The Pacific Ocean batters Central Coast headlands, fills bays, and floods river mouths, creating many coastal habitats, including sand dunes. Waves deposit sand on beaches and westerly winds blow it inland, where it catches on a drift line of vegetation and gradually forms a barrier of dunes. Over time, a mat of vegetation stabilizes the dunes and continues to trap blowing sand, increasing their size. The side of the dunes facing the ocean is usually sparsely vegetated, while the back side, protected from the wind, may have low shrubs and even trees. Dunes may also shelter lagoons, creating a protected environment for shorebirds and waterfowl.

The dunes at Salinas River (Site 99), Pismo Beach (Site 110) and Nipomo (Site 111) are part of the most extensive coastal dune system on the Pacific Coast; some are more than 500 feet tall, the highest coastal dunes in the western United States. The dunes may seem inhospitable but they support abundant wildlife, ranging from lizards, mice, and songbirds to rabbits, hawks, and deer. California least terns, Smith's blue butterflies, and Morro Bay kangaroo rats, all endangered, reproduce in the dunes and wintering monarch butterflies cluster on nearby trees. From the dunes, watch offshore for southern sea otters and gray whales.

Upper Left: southern sea otter
Lower Left: black-necked stilt and snowy plovers
Right: monarch butterfly
Illustration: Del Rio-Price and Charly Price

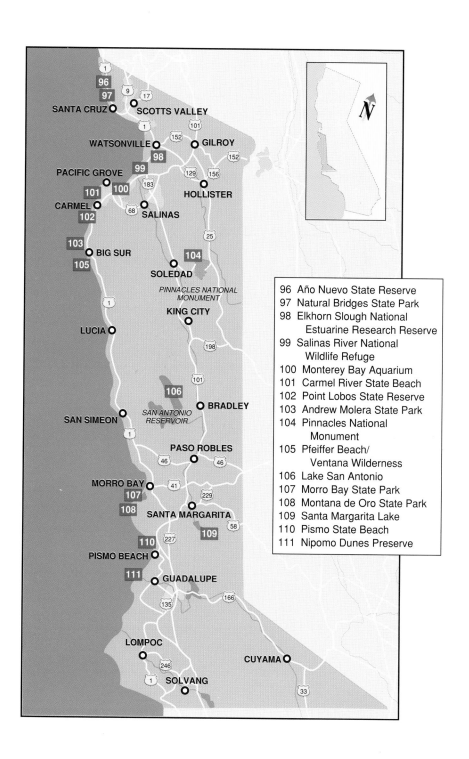

96 Año Nuevo State Reserve
97 Natural Bridges State Park
98 Elkhorn Slough National
   Estuarine Research Reserve
99 Salinas River National
   Wildlife Refuge
100 Monterey Bay Aquarium
101 Carmel River State Beach
102 Point Lobos State Reserve
103 Andrew Molera State Park
104 Pinnacles National
    Monument
105 Pfeiffer Beach/
    Ventana Wilderness
106 Lake San Antonio
107 Morro Bay State Park
108 Montana de Oro State Park
109 Santa Margarita Lake
110 Pismo State Beach
111 Nipomo Dunes Preserve

96 AÑO NUEVO STATE RESERVE

Description: Northern and central California's most important seal and sea lion rookery is a windswept world of sand dunes, surf-resistant mudstone ridges, and massive black mounds built by polychaete worms. The main attractions are the spectacular battles, birthing, breeding, and molting of the two-ton northern elephant seals. California and Steller sea lions breed on Año Nuevo Island. Offshore waters include gray whales, northern fur seals, and sea otters, listed as threatened in the southern end of their range. Also watch for loons, grebes, marbled murrelets, and seven gull species. Tidepools sustain more than 300 species of invertebrates and migratory shorebirds are abundant. A freshwater pond and brushy uplands attract waterfowl, songbirds, birds of prey, Santa Cruz salamanders and San Francisco garter snakes, both endangered.

Viewing Information: More than 250 bird species, many accidentals. High probability of seeing waterfowl, songbirds, and shorebirds in fall and spring, marine birds in winter. Elephant seals can be seen fighting, breeding, birthing, and weaning from December through March; molting occurs from April through August. Moderate probability of seeing sea lions in spring and summer, whales in December and January, March and April. Visitor center. Winter elephant seal viewing by tour only; handicap-accessible tours. Call for reservations in November.

Directions: Take Highway 1 twenty-five miles south of Half Moon Bay to entrance.

Ownership: DPR (415) 879-0595
Size: 1,200 acres   **Closest Town:** Pescadero

Año Nuevo is the only mainland breeding site in California used by northern elephant seals. Guided tours allow spectacular views of bulls fighting for dominance, protecting their harems, and breeding, and females nursing their pups. RICHARD A. BUCICH

Description: A wave-sculpted sandstone bridge, rocky tidepools, and sandy beach create a dramatic setting for one of the United State's largest monarch butterfly wintering sites, attracting about 100,000 butterflies annually. Monarchs pass the winter clustered on eucalyptus trees and are easily viewed on guided tours from the Monarch Trail boardwalk. The Milkweed Patch offers a close look at developing chrysalises and caterpillars. Secret Lagoon, a tranquil rainwater marsh, attracts mallards, great blue herons, green herons, and red-winged blackbirds. Tidepool tours reveal sea stars, tunicates, sponges, and other marine life. Watch offshore for cormorants, gulls, American black oystercatchers, brown pelicans, harbor seals, even occasional sea otters.

Viewing Information: Butterflies are seen from October through February. Tidepools provide excellent viewing at low tide. Look for wading birds and marine birds year-round; high probability of seeing waterfowl in winter and spring. Visitor center. Make tour reservations. *DO NOT TOUCH BUTTERFLIES OR CHRYSALISES. WATCH FOR POISON OAK. DON'T DISTURB TIDEPOOL LIFE. DANGEROUS SURF AND SLIPPERY ROCKS.*

Directions: In Santa Cruz, drive north on Highway 1 (Mission Street). Turn left on Swift Street, right on Delaware, then left on Swanton. Parking outside entry and within park.

Ownership: DPR (408) 423-4609
Size: Sixteen acres **Closest Town:** Santa Cruz

Most people visit Natural Bridges because of its remarkable views of monarch butterflies. Those who head for the beach are treated to guided tours that explore the flora and fauna of rock-bound tidepools inhabited by starfish, anemones, and other marine life. GEORGE WARD

98 ELKHORN SLOUGH NATIONAL ESTUARINE RESEARCH RESERVE

Description: Rolling hills with coastal live oak and Monterey pine overlook tidal creeks and restored salt marshes in this outstanding Monterey Bay wetland, one of nineteen national estuarine research reserves. Red-shouldered hawks, black-shouldered kites, and northern harriers hunt uplands favored by black-tailed deer. The Five Fingers Loop Overlook is nearly surrounded by water and shorebirds, including marbled godwits, ruddy turnstones, and western sandpipers. Trees along the South Marsh Loop shelter acorn woodpeckers and spring-arriving hummingbirds, tree swallows, and yellow-rumped warblers. Monterey pines serve as a rookery for great blue herons and great egrets. The marshes offer excellent views of common goldeneyes and buffleheads; deep water attracts double-crested cormorants, red-throated loons, ospreys, and brown pelicans, endangered on the West Coast. In spring and summer, pause on a boardwalk to watch the feeding behavior of leopard and smooth-hound sharks. Look for harbor seals and sea otters in the main slough channels.

Viewing Information: More than 250 bird species; more than 115 species have been seen at one spot, on one fall day. High probability of seeing waterfowl, wading birds, and shorebirds in fall and winter, marine birds in winter. Look for songbirds in fall and spring; birds of prey are seen year-round. High probability of seeing sharks feeding in spring and summer. Estuary an important fish nursery. Many trails, paved overlook. Tours available. Visitor center.

Directions: *North of Moss Landing on Highway 1, take Dolan Road east 3.5 miles to Elkhorn Road. Turn left and drive 2.2 miles to entrance.*

Ownership: DFG (408) 728-2822
Size: 1,400 acres   **Closest Town:** Monterey

Wintering ruddy turnstones are common at coastal sandy beaches, where they use their short, stout bills to turn over stones, shells, and kelp in search of small invertebrates.

B. "MOOSE" PETERSON

Description: This estuary wetland is located within the Pacific Coast's most extensive dune system. The two-mile trail to the beach passes grasslands and a dune-sheltered brackish lagoon favored by great blue herons, western sandpipers, and waterfowl. The dunes, stabilized by flowering plants, are inhabited by black legless lizards, song sparrows, and the endangered Smith's blue butterfly, which lays its eggs and feeds among the buckwheat. Follow the beach north to the river mouth; from April to June, snowy plovers nest in areas protected by mesh exclosures. Small river islands attract nesting American avocets, black-necked stilts, and gadwalls; gulls, terns, grebes, cormorants, and brown pelicans fish the estuary. Take the river trail back through grasslands hunted by black-shouldered kites, northern harriers, and short-eared owls.

Viewing Information: Nearly 200 bird species. Birds of prey and marine birds are seen year-round. Look for shorebirds from October to April. Moderate probability of seeing waterfowl from December through March, pelicans from spring through fall. An unimproved site. Interpretive dune boardwalk at nearby Marina Beach; wheelchair accessible. *DIRT ACCESS ROAD IMPASSABLE AFTER RAIN. PLEASE, NO WALKING ON DUNES.*

Directions: *From Monterey, drive north on Highway 1 eleven miles to Del Monte exit. Turn west and follow short dirt road to parking area.*

Ownership: USFWS (510) 792-0222
Size: 518 acres   **Closest Town:** Monterey

Most of the snowy plover's California nesting habitat has been permanently lost to coastal development. Snowy plovers require barren, sandy areas free of disturbance, where they build a nest that is no more than a slight depression in the sand. Speckled eggs blend perfectly with the sand. This youngster's coloration allows it to hide simply by standing still.

MIKE DANZENBAKER

100 | MONTEREY BAY AQUARIUM

Description: One of the world's greatest aquariums has more than 100 habitat exhibits and 6,500 examples of Monterey Bay marine life. Sea water is circulated through the Kelp Forest, the tallest aquarium in the world, where schools of fish and occasional divers move among a swaying kelp canopy. A wide range of bay habitats are explored at the 326,000-gallon Monterey Bay Habitat exhibit. The Sandy Shore's recreated shoreline includes an aviary filled with shorebirds; the Rocky Shore exhibit's anemone and limpet-encrusted rock is occasionally battered by waves. Sea otters dive and tumble in a 55,000-gallon, two-story exhibit with underwater views; life-size replicas of other marine mammals hang overhead. Touch pools invite visitors to touch everything from decorator crabs to bat rays. Outdoor decks wrap around the Great Tide Pool, where wild otters make frequent visits. Monterey Bay, one of the most diverse marine regions in the world, has been designated a National Marine Sanctuary.

Viewing Information: Excellent viewing year-round; all handicap-accessible. Street parking; parking lots.

Directions: From south of Monterey on Highway 1, take Del Monte Avenue/Pacific Grove exit. Follow signs through tunnel to aquarium. From north, on Highway 1, take Fremont Street exit. Turn right, travel to Del Monte Avenue and turn left, following signs through tunnel to aquarium.

Ownership: Monterey Bay Aquarium Foundation (408) 648-4926
Size: 2.2 acres   **Closest Town:** Monterey

Monterey Bay Aquarium has more than one hundred innovative galleries and exhibits, with over 6,000 "residents." Huge pumps circulate sea water through the twenty-eight foot-tall, 335,000-gallon Kelp Forest, the world's tallest aquarium. Divers swim among the fronds of undulating kelp, hand-feeding fish and talking directly with the viewers.

MONTEREY BAY AQUARIUM

Description: The Carmel River flows into the Carmel River Bird Sanctuary's brackish lagoon, cuts through a wide sandy beach, and empties into coastal waters that are part of an underwater ecological reserve and sea otter refuge. Lush grasses and vegetation border the river mouth lagoon, which draws migratory gulls, waterfowl, and shorebirds. Resident great egrets, great blue herons, and black-crowned night herons fish in the shallows. Spring-arriving songbirds inhabit the riparian border. The underwater reserve, extending from Pescadero Point to Point Lobos, gives divers a view of kelp, California hydrocoral, sea anemones, and other marine life. Watch offshore for occasional harbor seals, gray whales, and sea otters.

Viewing Information: High probability of seeing waterfowl and shorebirds in fall and winter. Marine birds and wading birds are seen year-round. *BEACH UNSAFE FOR SWIMMING. NO COLLECTING IN UNDERWATER RESERVE.*

Directions: *In Carmel, on Highway 1, turn west on Rio Road. Drive to Santa Lucia Street and turn left. Travel five blocks and turn left on Carmelo Sreet. Drive .4 mile to parking area.*

Ownership: DPR (408) 624-4909
Size: 105 acres **Closest Town:** Carmel

A threatened species, the southern sea otter is most often seen in Central Coast waters among a bed of kelp. While floating on its back, the otter opens a sea urchin by pounding it against a rock held on its stomach. A light bundle of fluffy fur on its belly may be a dozing otter pup. ART WOLFE

102 POINT LOBOS STATE RESERVE

Description: Named for the "sea wolves," or sea lions that haul out on the offshore rocks, this rugged point features meadows, forested headlands, sheltered coves, rocky tidepools, and beaches. The Cypress Grove Trail passes mounded dusky woodrat houses as it weaves through a world-famous Monterey cypress grove. Carmelo Meadow offers glimpses of black-tailed deer, brush rabbits, even bobcats. Harbor seals, sea lions, sea otters, and gray whales swim the waters off Sea Lion Point. The South Shore Trail leads past rocky inlets with killdeer, sandpipers, and black oystercatchers to the Bird Island Overlook, where the outer rocks shelter up to 2,000 nesting Brandt's cormorants. Watch for sea otters and harbor seals at Whaler's Cove, where divers can explore kelp beds, sea stars, and other marine life in an underwater ecological reserve.

Viewing Information: More than 150 bird species. High probability of seeing shorebirds, sea otters, and harbor seals year-round; marine birds in spring and summer. Look for sea lions from August through May, gray whales from January to March. Occasional porpoises. Guided tours. *DANGEROUS SURF. SEE DIVING REGULATIONS. NO COLLECTING. WATCH FOR POISON OAK.*

Directions: *From Carmel on Highway 1, drive south 3.5 miles to park entrance.*

Ownership: DPR (408) 624-4909
Size: 1,304 acres   **Closest Town:** Carmel

Wind, surf, and time have sculpted the bold headlands, irregular coves, and secluded beaches at Pt. Lobos, where stunning scenery is also remarkable wildlife habitat. Sea otters, seals, and sea lions appear in sheltered coves, while offshore rocks host huge sea bird colonies. Watch offshore for gray whales. CHUCK PLACE

Description: The Big Sur River descends through redwoods, pines, oaks, and madrones, then meanders by grasslands and meadows before entering the Pacific Ocean at Molera Point. The Headlands Trail overlooks offshore rocks populated by western gulls, Brandt's cormorants, harbor seals, and sea lions. Sea otters float among rafts of kelp and gray whales pass by offshore. Red-necked phalaropes and black turnstones feed on a two-mile beach below marine terraces and meadows that attract black-tailed deer and a dozen species of birds of prey. Streamside trails offer glimpses of bobcats, raccoons, gray foxes, western screech owls, American dippers, belted kingfishers, and great blue herons. Seven species of snake inhabit the park, ranging from aquatic garter snakes to western rattlesnakes. Hummingbirds, swallows, warblers, and vireos appear seasonally.

Viewing Information: Nearly 200 bird species. Marine birds and birds of prey are seen year-round, highest viewing probability in winter. Also look for shorebirds and waterfowl in winter, songbirds in spring and summer. Marine mammals are seen year-round. Watch for gray whales from end of Headlands Trail, late December through February. Primitive walk-in campground. Equestrian trails. *DANGEROUS SURF, POISON OAK, TICKS.*

Directions: *From Carmel on Highway 1, travel twenty-one miles south to entrance.*

Ownership: DPR (408) 667-2316
Size: 4,786 acres **Closest Town:** Carmel

California brown pelican populations have been jeopardized by the ingestion of DDT and other toxins consumed in their prey; the toxins caused thin-shelled eggs that broke during incubation. The endangered pelican is now recovering, and is fairly common along the entire coastline. Brown pelicans are known for acrobatic fishing methods and a bulging neck pouch.

RICHARD A. BUCICH

The trained "seal" at zoos and circuses, the California sea lion is a natural performer. They can be spotted anywhere along California's rocky beaches, sometimes tossing objects or swimming playfully in the water. They are consummate divers, remaining at depths of over 400 feet for twenty minutes.   TOM & PAT LEESON

Description: Rugged volcanic spires and crags cloaked by chaparral and digger pines rise abruptly from oak-studded hills. This pristine area sustains a dozen lizard species and half as many snakes, including coast horned lizards, western whiptails, California king snakes, and gopher snakes. In late summer and fall, watch roads and trails for legions of slow-moving tarantulas on the move to find a mate. Oak woodlands and riparian corridors shelter black-tailed deer and gray foxes. Spring brings abundant wildflowers and millions of swarming lady bird beetles. Prairie falcons and American kestrels hunt from rocky perches on the Balconies Cliffs. Dozens of turkey vultures roost in trees near visitor center, flying off in dramatic morning and evening departures. California thrashers, black-headed grosbeaks, and Nuttall's woodpeckers are common.

Viewing Information: Look for birds of prey from January to July. Songbirds are seen year-round, best viewing in spring. High probability of seeing reptiles, deer, and gray foxes year-round. More than 600 plants. Watch for tule elk and pronghorn antelope south of monument on Highway 25. Tarantulas, deer, feral pigs, and cattle on east side road in fall. *HIGHWAY 146 DOESN'T RUN THROUGH ENTIRE MONUMENT. WEST SIDE ROAD IS NARROW AND WINDING.*

Directions: *To east side visitor center: from Gilroy on Highway 101, take Highway 25 south forty-two miles to Highway 146, turn right, and drive five miles to visitor center. To west side: at Soledad on Highway 101, take Highway 146 east twelve miles to end of road.*

Ownership: NPS (408) 389-4485
Size: 16,000 acres   **Closest Town:** Hollister, King City

The rocky, arid environment at Pinnacles National Monument attracts many species normally associated with desert-like conditions. Every summer and fall, thousands of slow-moving tarantulas appear on roads and in the open, searching for a mate. While they are mostly harmless, these hairy arachnids should never be touched.

RICK McINTYRE

105 PFEIFFER BEACH/VENTANA WILDERNESS

Description: Big Sur's white sand coastline is marked by wave-sculpted blowholes and sea stacks populated by Brandt's cormorants, American black oystercatchers, and other birds. Scores of shorebirds feed on the beaches. In the spring and summer, endangered Smith's blue butterflies inhabit buckwheat on the coastal bluffs. From parking overlooks, watch nearshore waters for wintering loons and scoters and resident harbor seals, California sea lions, and sea otters; northern elephant seals and gray whales will be farther out. Several coast overlooks are bordered by the 165,000-acre Ventana Wilderness, where wildlife is abundant, including marbled murrelets, spotted owls, and endangered birds of prey.

Viewing Information: More than 200 bird species. Marine birds, shorebirds, and brown pelicans are seen year-round; best viewing in winter. Look for waterfowl in winter. Moderate probability of seeing birds of prey, marine mammals, deer, and small mammals year-round; peregrine falcons in spring and summer. High probability of seeing songbirds in spring and summer. Watch for gray whales from December to April. Marbled murrelets and spotted owls nest among redwoods. Enter Ventana Wilderness at Big Sur Station.

Directions: From Pfeiffer/Big Sur State Park, drive .75 mile south on Highway 1 to Sycamore Canyon Road. Turn west and drive two miles to parking. Several paved vista points farther south, on Highway 1.

Ownership: USFS (408) 667-2423, (408) 385-5434
Size: 165,000 acres   **Closest Town:** Big Sur

Even crashing surf can't conceal the American black oystercatcher's loud, piercing call. This unusual shorebird was named for its love of oysters. It easily opens the shell by inserting its broad, stout bill before the oyster can close, or the bird will batter the shell until it opens.   ART WOLFE

Description: Sixteen miles long, this enormous lake features a resident herd of more than 400 black-tailed deer, up to 100,000 migratory waterfowl, and the largest wintering population of bald eagles in central and southern California. More than fifty bald eagles, twelve resident golden eagles, and ospreys roost on shoreline snags. The best viewing is from the county's large tour boat, which provides information and binoculars. In the spring, golden eagles nest in trees near the shore. Canada Geese, Clark's and western grebes, white pelicans, wood ducks, and herons gather on the lake; miles of muddy shoreline are probed by American avocets and killdeer. Resident acorn woodpeckers, turkeys, and California quail are joined by many migrants, including California thrashers, cedar waxwings, and yellow-billed magpies.

Viewing Information: 100 bird species. High probability of seeing eagles and other birds of prey from December 15 to March 10. Also see waterfowl in winter, white pelicans from fall through early summer. Look for songbirds in spring and summer. Deer, bobcats, and squirrels are seen year-round. Boat tours, fee, reservations required; see phone number below. Visitor Center.

Directions: *From north of King City on Highway 101, take Jolon Road/G-14 exit west twenty-four miles. Go right on Interlake Road. After twelve miles, turn right to lake on San Antonio Road. Drive four miles to lake. Or from Paso Robles on Highway 101, take Lake Nacimiento exit. Turn left on Highway 46/G-14. Follow G-14 for twenty-six miles to San Antonio Road and turn right.*

Ownership: Monterey County Water Resources Agency (805) 472-2311
Size: 25,000 acres   **Closest Town:** King City

Mule deer are common throughout the state. They may feed at night, in the early morning, and the late afternoon, but they usually bed down during the day. They are easy to spot at Lake San Antonio, where they browse without concern in meadows and clearings, though they are never far from cover.

GARY R. ZAHM

107 MORRO BAY STATE PARK

Description: This rich estuary includes creekside wetlands, salt marsh sloughs, open water, eel grass beds, and Morro Rock, a reserve for endangered peregrine falcons. The park museum offers views of thousands of migratory loons, buffleheads, wigeons, and northern pintails; resident cormorants, white and brown pelicans are mixed among the group. More than 10,000 wintering black brant feed in the eel grass, a haven for fish such as halibut and jacksmelt. Harbor seals, sea lions, and sea otters appear along the bay. Gulls and terns circle over mudflats with legions of sanderlings, willets, and other shorebirds. Watch for great blue herons, great egrets, and black-crowned night herons at the nature preserve; nesting herons share nearby eucalyptus trees with monarch butterflies, hummingbirds, even red-shouldered hawks.

Viewing Information: More than 400 birds species in county. Waterfowl and songbirds are seen year-round; best viewed in winter. High probability of seeing shorebirds from fall through spring, marine birds and wading birds year-round. Herons nest from January to July. Look for marine mammals, deer, and small mammals year-round. Excellent car and boat viewing; many trails.

Directions: From San Luis Obispo on Highway 1, take Highway 1 north to Los Osos/ Baywood Park exit. Turn left on South Bay Boulevard, following signs to park.

Ownership:DPR (805) 772-2694
Size: 4,000 acres **Closest Town:** Morro Bay

Morro Bay's wetlands, salt marsh, and sandy beaches give way to dramatic views of Morro Rock, a protected reserve for nesting American peregrine falcons.

ED COOPER

108 MONTANA DE ORO STATE PARK

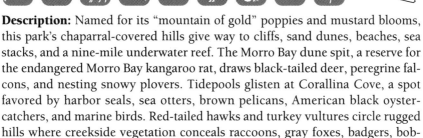

Description: Named for its "mountain of gold" poppies and mustard blooms, this park's chaparral-covered hills give way to cliffs, sand dunes, beaches, sea stacks, and a nine-mile underwater reef. The Morro Bay dune spit, a reserve for the endangered Morro Bay kangaroo rat, draws black-tailed deer, peregrine falcons, and nesting snowy plovers. Tidepools glisten at Corallina Cove, a spot favored by harbor seals, sea otters, brown pelicans, American black oyster-catchers, and marine birds. Red-tailed hawks and turkey vultures circle rugged hills where creekside vegetation conceals raccoons, gray foxes, badgers, bobcats, even mountain lions. Monarch butterflies winter here.

Viewing Information: High probability of seeing shorebirds and wading birds year-round, waterfowl in winter. Look for birds of prey and marine birds in spring, songbirds in fall. Seals, otters, and land mammals may be seen year-round. Horses okay, but no dogs on trails. *DANGEROUS SURF.*

Directions: *From San Luis Obispo, take Highway 1 north to the Los Osos/ Baywood exit. Turn left on South Bay Boulevard and continue 2.5 miles to Los Osos Valley Road. Turn right and drive 2.5 miles to entrance.*

Ownership: DPR (805) 528-0513
Size: 8,227 acres   **Closest Town:** Los Osos

109 SANTA MARGARITA LAKE

Description: Hills and cliffs border protected coves that shelter Canada geese, wood ducks, and other waterfowl. Abundant fish attract western gulls, Caspian's terns, white pelicans, and wintering ospreys and bald eagles. Look for egrets, herons, and belted kingfishers at marshy inlets. Golden eagles, northern goshawks, and ferruginous hawks ride updrafts near the cliffs. Black-tailed deer and occasional coyotes pass through oak grasslands that sustain California quail, acorn woodpeckers, and black phoebes.

Viewing Information: Birds of prey and wading birds are present year-round, waterfowl in fall and winter. Songbirds, deer, and small mammals are seen in spring and summer. Managed by San Luis Obispo County.

Directions: *Eight miles from Santa Margarita. Take Highway 101 to Highway 58 east through Santa Margarita. Turn right on Highway 58 (Estrada Road), following signs to Pozo Road. Continue straight on Pozo Road to Santa Margarita Lake Road and turn left. Drive one mile to entrance.*

Ownership: ACE (805) 438-5485
Size: 8,000 acres   **Closest Town:**Paso Robles

110 PISMO STATE BEACH

Description: This site features California's most extensive coastal sand dunes. Eucalyptus trees here shelter the nation's largest population of wintering monarch butterflies. Some years, nearly 200,000 monarchs cluster on trees at the North Beach Campground. Trails through the dune preserve bear the tracks of lizards, mice, jackrabbits, bobcats, and coyotes. Also found here is a showy plant, the giant coreopsis. Beavers reside in Meadow Creek, which widens into a lagoon favored by waterfowl. Fifty bird species may be seen here, including Audubon's warblers, long-billed marsh wrens, and black-crowned night herons. Shorebirds follow beach tides, searching for pismo clams. Offshore waters reveal resident harbor seals and sea otters; during winter, watch for humpbacked whales, endangered gray whales, and thousands of sooty shearwaters, a marine bird. Other endangered visitors include bald eagles, peregrine falcons, and least terns.

Viewing Information: Butterflies are abundant November through March. High probability of seeing shorebirds and songbirds year-round. Look for birds of prey year-round, bald eagles in winter. Waterfowl and marine birds are also common in winter. Beavers best viewed at dawn and dusk. *DUNE VEGETATION IS FRAGILE.*

Directions: *From Pismo Beach on Highway 1, drive south one mile to North Beach Campground.*

Ownership: DPR (805) 489-1869
Size: 800 acres   **Closest Town:** Pismo Beach

Monarch butterflies are feather-light travelers that navigate thousands of miles to trees along the Central Coast. Here, huge clusters of butterflies gather to rest and reproduce. As the sun warms them, the underside of their fluttering wings flash silver and the trees seem to vibrate with pulsing lights.

ERWIN & PEGGY BAUER

Description: California's most extensive coastal sand dunes include the highest beach dunes in the western United States, with some over 500 feet tall. The dunes are stabilized by stunted vegetation, including at least eighteen protected plants. Black-shouldered kites, Cooper's hawks, and northern harriers cruise over dune swales and ridges inhabited by coast garter snakes, California quail, black-tailed deer, and coyotes. Least terns—endangered in California—nest south of the Santa Maria River and fish at the river mouth. Thousands of shorebirds, including nesting snowy plovers, scour the beaches while gulls, cormorants, loons, and brown pelicans remain offshore; some winters, they are joined by 500,000 sooty shearwaters. Inland lakes attract ospreys, terns, and scores of wintering waterfowl, including tundra swans, white pelicans, mallards, and ruddy ducks.

Viewing Information: More than 200 bird species. Look for waterfowl in winter, pelicans from July through November. Marine birds are seen year-round, shorebirds in winter. See least terns from April through August. Birds of prey are seen year-round. Wildflowers are abundant in March. *DO NOT DISTURB LEAST TERN NESTING SITES.*

Directions: From Guadalupe on Highway 1, take West Main Street (Highway 166) west five miles. Pass entrance gate and continue 1.5 miles to preserve.

Ownership: Santa Barbara County; TNC, (805) 545-9925
Size: 3,417 acres   **Closest Town:** Santa Maria

Ruddy ducks are common at wetlands and the male, pictured here in breeding plumage, is easy to identify. Ruddy ducks are much more at home in the water than in the air. To fly, the ducks must patter awkwardly across the water before taking off.
RICHARD A. BUCICH

Sleek-bodied grebes are excellent divers and subsist on a diet of fish. Grebes also consume their own feathers, probably to help pad sharp fish bones as they are digested.

SOUTH COAST

Habitat Loss

Intense development, dams, and water diversions have eliminated, degraded, or seriously fragmented wildlife habitat. River flows are seasonal and associated riparian forests are reduced. Most of the southern wetlands have been lost to coastal development. Homes and businesses have nearly eliminated the once-dominant coastal sage scrub habitat.

Though diminished in numbers, wildlife tenaciously persist and concentrate at remaining beaches, wetlands, riparian corridors, and uplands, which are often vigorously protected. At least eight species are endangered due to loss of habitat. A remnant population of unarmored threespine stickleback inhabit a few, clear stream pools in the San Gabriel Mountains. Manmade wetland islands safeguard nesting habitat for California least terns. Least Bell's vireos persist inland, at a few remnant riparian areas.

Left: Least Bell's vireo
Upper Right: Unarmored threespine stickleback
Lower Right: California brown pelican
Illustration: Del Rio-Price and Charly Price

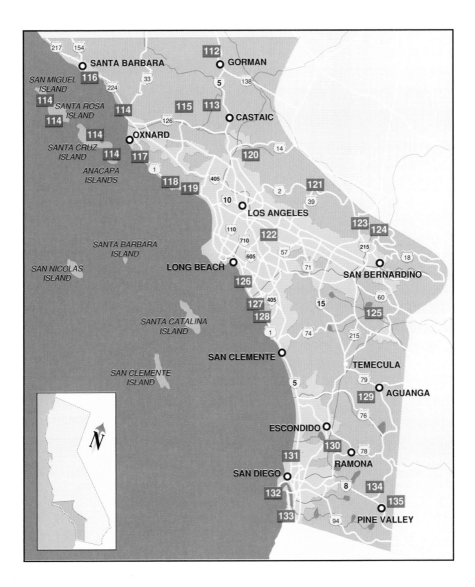

112 Mount Pinos Observation Point
113 Piru Creek
114 Channel Islands National Park
115 Sespe Condor Sanctuary
116 Carpinteria State Beach
117 Point Mugu State Park
118 Malibu Creek State Park and Lagoon
119 Topanga State Park
120 Western San Gabriel Driving Loop
121 Jarvi Bighorn Sheep Vista
122 Whittier Narrows Nature Center
123 Rim of the World Scenic
        Byway Tour
124 Silverwood Lake

125 San Jacinto Wildlife Area
126 Bolsa Chica Ecological Reserve
127 Upper Newport Bay Ecological
        Reserve and Regional Park
128 Crystal Cove State Park
129 Palomar Mountain State Park
130 Blue Sky Ecological Reserve
131 Torrey Pines State Reserve/
        Los Penasquitos Marsh
132 Cabrillo National Monument
133 Tijuana Slough National
        Estuarine Research Reserve
134 Cuyamaca Rancho State Park
135 Laguna Mountain Recreation Area

112 MOUNT PIÑOS OBSERVATION POINT

Description: This summit overlook provides panoramic views of the greater Los Angeles Basin. The parking lot, a small meadow, and trails laden with pine needles offer glimpses of lodgepole chipmunks, mountain quail, and band-tailed pigeons. The forest canopy shelters mountain bluebirds, Clark's nut-crackers, Nuttall's and hairy woodpeckers, and five owl species, including spotted, screech, and flammulated owls. Northern goshawks nest among the conifers. Watch the skies for endangered California condors and Andean condors, which have been released at the nearby Sespe Condor Sanctuary.

Viewing Information: Birds of prey, upland birds, and small mammals are seen year-round, best viewed in spring and summer. Look for songbirds in spring and summer, band-tailed pigeons in fall. Low to moderate probability of seeing condors in late summer. Short dirt road leads to summit; *ROAD IM-PASSABLE WHEN WET.*

Directions: *From Frazier Park/Interstate 5, take Mount Piños Recreation Area exit west twenty miles to Chula Vista parking area.*

Ownership: USFS (805) 681-2764
Size: Three acres **Closest Town:** Frazier Park

113 PIRU CREEK

Description: Pyramid Lake empties into pristine Piru Creek, which flows eighteen miles before funneling into Piru Lake. Float downstream into a tranquil riparian canyon fringed by chaparral, cottonwoods, and rugged rock formations scored by ribbons of quartz. Watch for black bears, raccoons, and bobcats near the banks; occasional ospreys, belted kingfishers, and cormorants fish here for rainbow trout. Red-tailed hawks and golden eagles hunt from the streamside canopy, which shelters bats and songbirds. Stop at Pyramid Lake to spot herons, egrets, western pond turtles, mallards, and other waterfowl. Watch near the lakes for Andean condors and reintroduced California condors.

Viewing Information: Predators, small mammals, and birds of prey are seen year-round. High probability of seeing waterfowl in winter, wading birds and songbirds in spring and summer. Two waterfalls on creek must be portaged. Trail borders creek for three miles.

Directions: *North of Castaic on Interstate 5, take Templin Highway exit and turn left. At Old Highway 99, turn right and drive five miles to Frenchman's Flat.*

Ownership: USFS (805) 296-9710
Size: Eighteen miles **Closest Town:** Castaic

Description: Five rocky, wave-blasted islands are encircled by the rich habitat of a National Marine Sanctuary. The islands are crucial rookeries for California sea lions, harbor seals, northern elephant seals, northern fur seals, and threatened Steller sea lions and Guadalupe fur seals. Rugged cliffs and scrub-dominated plateaus provide critical habitat for sixty bird species, including Cassin's auklets, Xantus' murrelets, pigeon guillemots, ashy storm petrels, Brandt's cormorants, and western gulls. Endangered brown pelicans also nest here. Craggy shorelines include tidepools inhabited by turban snails, tube worms, and limpets. The islands offer views of up to twenty species of whales, porpoises, and dolphins, some of which can be seen from a visitor center in Ventura. Many plant and wildlife species here, such as gray foxes and scrub jays, differ from their mainland counterparts and are considered distinct subspecies.

Viewing Information: More than sixty breeding bird species. High probability of seeing marine birds year-round, especially in spring. Seals and sea lions are seen year-round. Also watch for humpbacked and pilot whales, seven dolphin species, small mammals, predators, songbirds, and amphibians year-round. Gray whales and northern elephant seals are seen in winter. Trails, camping, picnic areas on islands; boat tours from Ventura.

Directions: *From north of Ventura on Highway 101, take Victoria Avenue exit and turn left. Turn right on Olivas Adobe Road. Take Spinnaker Drive to visitor center. Or from south of Ventura on Highway 101, take Seaward Avenue exit. Turn left on Harbor Boulevard and turn onto Spinnaker Drive.*

Ownership: NPS (805) 658-5730, (805) 658-5700
Size: 250,000 acres   **Closest Town:** Ventura

These wave-battered and sculpted rocks are near East Anacapa Island, one of the five islands included in Channel Islands National Park. The isolated islands are surrounded by a rich marine environment that attracts a half-dozen species of breeding seals and sea lions, as well as nearly a dozen breeding sea birds.

J.C. LEACOCK

115 SESPE CONDOR SANCTUARY

Description: The steep chaparral and forested slopes of this rugged backcountry sanctuary seventy-five miles from Los Angeles are now home to two reintroduced, endangered California condors and one companion pair of non-native Andean condors. This release site and adjacent country are the only places in the world to see wild California condors. Every year, project cooperators hope to release additional adults from the growing brood raised during the ten-year captive breeding program. The condors, the largest land birds in North America with a wingspan of more than nine feet, are joined by occasional golden eagles, prairie falcons, and reintroduced peregrine falcons. Black bears are common in the sanctuary.

Viewing Information: Viewing is good year-round. An adult California condor has white triangles on the underside of each wing, visible in flight. It has a turkey-like red wattle on the face and is much smaller than its Andean cousin.

Directions: *From Interstate 5, drive west on Highway 126 to Fillmore. Drive north on A Street (Highway 4) four miles and turn right at road to Sespe Oil Field. Drive three miles, passing the Oak Flat Forest Service Station, and continue north for about ten miles to Dough Flat Viewpoint.*

Ownership: USFS (805) 683-6711
Size: 53,000 acres   **Closest Town:** Fillmore

North America's largest land bird, the California condor soars in easy and graceful flight, powered by wings that span nine feet. Loss of habitat, poisoning, and slow maturity and reproduction rates reduced condor numbers to just a handful in 1987. In 1991, a successful captive breeding program released two birds to the wild at Sespe Condor Sanctuary.

JEFF FOOTT

116 | CARPINTERIA STATE BEACH

Description: Carpinteria Creek's riparian woodland gives way to a tidal lagoon bordered by a sandbar and a rocky reef riddled with tidepools. These pristine pools are inhabited by chitons, periwinkles, sea anemones, sea stars, and other marine life. A small beach east of the tidepools is a major haul out for harbor seals, particularly at night.

Viewing Information: Viewing at tidepools is best at low tide. Seals can be seen year-round. Guided tours. Indoor tidepool at visitor center. *WATCH WAVES, SLIPPERY ROCKS. NO COLLECTING.*

Directions: *At Carpinteria on Highway 101, take Casitas Pass Road exit. Turn right on Carpinteria Avenue. Turn left on Palm Avenue and continue to entrance.*

Ownership: DPR (805) 684-2811
Size: Eighty-four acres   **Closest Town:** Carpinteria

117 | POINT MUGU STATE PARK

Description: This park located at the edge of the Santa Monica Mountains encompasses five miles of sandy coastline, rocky bluffs, native grasslands, and unspoiled backcountry accessible only on foot or by horse. At Sycamore Cove and La Jolla Beach, watch for gulls, cormorants, shorebirds, and brown pelicans and least terns, both endangered in California. Year-round populations of harbor seals, California sea lions, and common dolphins are joined by migratory gray whales. Monarch butterflies cluster on trees at Sycamore Canyon Campground; look here and near the creek for Nuttall's woodpeckers, California thrashers, and many songbirds. The rugged, 6,000-acre Boney Mountain Wilderness Area sustains resident mule deer, gray foxes, skunks, even mountain lions. Bats roost among the sycamores, a spring destination for breeding flycatchers, hummingbirds, and wrens.

Viewing Information: More than 200 bird species. Marine, wading birds, and songbirds are seen year-round; songbirds in April and May, September and October. High probability of seeing shorebirds from August through April, whales from December to April. Watch marine birds from Mugu Rock. Excellent whale watching at Point Dume State Park.

Directions: *From Oxnard on Highway 1, drive south twelve miles to entrance.*

Ownership: DPR (818) 706-1310
Size: 13,925 acres   **Closest Town:** Oxnard

118　MALIBU CREEK STATE PARK AND LAGOON

Description: Chaparral-covered hills and steep, wooded canyons give way to oak-studded grasslands and meandering streams that end at Malibu Lagoon, one of Los Angeles' few remaining estuaries. Raccoons, coyotes, gray foxes, badgers, and mountain lions live in rough backcountry patrolled by Cooper's hawks and golden eagles; the eagles nest in the park. Moist, rocky gorges with ferns and orchids shelter canyon wrens and white-throated swifts. Lazuli buntings, warbling vireos, and Swainson's thrushes live among the trees that shade Malibu Creek, which supports California's southernmost steelhead spawning run. Watch for buffleheads, ring-necked ducks, and belted kingfishers at the creek and Century Lake. Malibu Lagoon State Beach, a brackish marsh that attracts more than 200 bird species, is also a nursery for many fish, and is home to reintroduced tidewater gobies.

Viewing Information: Birds of prey, wading birds, songbirds, predators, and deer are seen year-round; songbirds in April and May, September and October. High probability of seeing waterfowl, gulls, and shorebirds in fall and winter; terns in summer and fall. Hike or ride horses on trails; some connect to nearby Topanga State Park. Visitor centers.

Directions: From Calabasas on Highway 101, drive west to Las Virgenes exit; from exit, drive south three miles to entrance. To reach Lagoon, from Santa Monica on Highway 1, drive north twelve miles to entrance.

Ownership: DPR (818) 706-8809, (818) 706-1310
Size: 7,169 acres　**Closest Town:** Calabasas, Malibu (Lagoon)

The brilliant coloration of the male lazuli bunting helps attract a drab, grayish-brown mate. Its fluttering descent to the ground is part of a court-ship ritual that seals the union.

JEFF FOOTT

Description: This pristine park on the edge of the Santa Monica Mountains is the largest U.S. wildland within a city boundary. Adjacent private and public wildlands provide landscape corridors for park wildlife and increase the size of this urban wilderness to 16,000 acres. More than thirty miles of trails traverse slopes of oak-studded meadows, chaparral, and forested canyons. Desert cottontails, California quail, scrub jays, coyotes, badgers, and bobcats inhabit the open country. Southern mule deer browse among scrub and coastal live oaks that shelter acorn woodpeckers, Hutton's vireos, blue-gray gnatcatchers, and western screech owls. A 1.5-mile trail through rugged Santa Ynez Canyon passes a twenty-foot waterfall; stream orchids and tiger lilies bloom near California bays, sycamores, and willows, habitat favored by raccoons, canyon wrens, Swainson's thrushes, and warbling vireos.

Viewing Information: Songbirds, upland birds, predators, and deer are seen year-round; songbirds are abundant in spring and fall. Equestrian and nature trails. Visitor center. Tours. Linked to other parks by Backbone Trail.

Directions: *From Santa Monica, take Highway 1 north to Topanga Canyon Boulevard (Highway 27). Turn north and drive four miles. Take the Entrada exit and drive east to entrance.*

Ownership: DPR (213) 455-2465
Size: 8,769 acres **Closest Town:** Topanga

The badger, a relative of the skunk, otter, and weasel, has long claws for digging burrows. It is protected from other predators by dense fur, tough hide, a strong musk, and a repertoire of ferocious-sounding snarls, growls, and hisses. Badgers are one of a handful of animals that prey on rattlesnakes. JEFF FOOTT

120 WESTERN SAN GABRIEL DRIVING LOOP

Description: The auto tour begins at Soledad Campground, where an interpretive trail leads to the Santa Clara River with views of a tiny, endangered fish, the unarmored threespine stickleback. Drive through the mountain and desert habitats of Aliso Canyon, then enjoy Mount Gleason's breathtaking vistas. Spring wildflowers line the summit road and forest openings may reveal gray foxes, coyotes, or mule deer. Pines shelter brown towhees, great horned owls, and ten woodpecker species. The skies are scribed by red-tailed hawks, golden eagles, and occasional peregrine falcons. On the Santa Clara Divide Road, watch for Andean condors and reintroduced California condors. Tour ends at Placerita Canyon, where oak woodlands shelter acorn woodpeckers, band-tailed pigeons, and the usual squirrels and chipmunks.

Viewing Information: Birds of prey, woodpeckers, mammals, and fish can be seen year-round. Songbirds are abundant in spring and fall. Watch for condors early in morning. Allow four hours for loop. Mount Gleason area closed in winter. Sites on Pacific Crest Trail. *THIS IS A NARROW, DANGEROUS ROAD WITH MANY BLIND TURNS. SOUND HORN AS YOU APPROACH CURVES AND LISTEN FOR HORNS OF ONCOMING TRAFFIC.*

Directions: *From Los Angeles, take Highway 14 north to Shadow Pines exit and turn right on Soledad Canyon Road. Drive five miles to Soledad picnic area. Continue 9.7 miles to Aliso Canyon Road, turn right, and drive 7.2 miles to Angeles Forest Highway. Turn right and drive 2.8 miles to Santa Clara Divide Road (FS Road 3N17) and turn right toward Mount Gleason. This intermittently paved road reaches the summit in nine miles, then continues twenty-two miles to Sand Canyon Road. Turn right here, drive 2.8 miles to Placerita Canyon Road and turn left. Drive five miles to junction with Highway 14.*

Ownership: USFS (818) 899-1900
Size: Sixty-four-mile loop   **Closest Town:** Santa Clarita

California ground squirrels are conspicuous residents at parks and wildlands, leaving thier underground burrows all day to feed on plants, nuts, or other edibles left behind by park visitors. Enjoy these spunky mammals from a distance: the fleas they harbor often carry bubonic plague.

RICHARD A. BUCICH

121 JARVI BIGHORN SHEEP VISTA

Description: This rocky, wooded area covered with chaparral, oaks, and conifers adjoins the San Gabriel Wilderness and offers sweeping views of San Gabriel Canyon and the Twin Peaks. Early in the morning, watch for Nelson's bighorn sheep on the rocky ledges. Red-tailed hawks and ravens often glide on the mountain's thermal updrafts.

Viewing Information: Bring binoculars. While bighorns often are within 100 feet of highway pullout, they are well-camouflaged and take patience to see. Both rams and ewes have permanent horns; rams' are larger. Also watch for bighorns from Highway 2, near tunnels one mile west of this site; very limited parking. Good car viewing. PLEASE, DON'T DISTURB BIGHORNS.

Directions: A pull-out on Highway 2, about .25 mile west of the junction of highways 2 and 39.

Ownership: USFS (818) 790-1151
Size: .25 acre **Closest Town:** Wrightwood

122 WHITTIER NARROWS NATURE CENTER

Description: Trails crisscross this urban sanctuary bordered by the San Gabriel River. Desert cottontails, black-tailed jackrabbits, California thrashers, and northern flickers hop beneath sycamores and willows that shelter orange-crowned warblers, yellow-breasted chats, and black-headed and blue grosbeaks. Black-shouldered kites, Cooper's hawks, and other birds of prey roost in the upper canopy. In the fall, riparian growth hides ash-throated flycatchers, yellow-rumped warblers, and western kingbirds. Resident ospreys and several heron species fish in four lakes sought by thousands of northern pintails, canvasbacks, wood ducks, and teal. During spring, watch for white-faced ibis, black-chinned hummingbirds, and Nuttall's woodpeckers.

Viewing Information: Nearly 275 bird species. Birds of prey, wading birds, waterfowl, songbirds, and mammals are seen year-round. High probability of seeing waterfowl in fall and winter, songbirds from fall through spring. Also look for nesting kites and introduced northern cardinals. No car viewing; handicap-accessible nature trail. Museum. Observation blind.

Directions: From Highway 60, take Santa Anita Avenue exit south to Durfee Avenue and turn left. Follow Durfee Avenue to entrance.

Ownership: Los Angeles County (818) 444-1872
Size: 277 acres **Closest Town:** South El Monte

123 RIM OF THE WORLD SCENIC BYWAY TOUR

Description and Directions: This full-day tour begins and ends in the Los Angeles Basin and spans habitats ranging from desert and coastal valley to high-elevation forests and several lakes. Begin on Highway 138 two miles west of Interstate 15 at Mormon Rocks Station, where desert chaparral hides coastal horned lizards, California thrashers, and western kingbirds. Rugged cliffs here are favored by white-throated swifts and birds of prey. Follow Highway 138 east, over Interstate 15, and weave through Crowder Canyon, watching for golden eagles, red-tailed hawks, and coyotes. Stop at Silverwood Lake (site number 124 in this book), then climb through dense conifers that are home to gray squirrels, southern mule deer, turkeys, mountain quail, and acorn woodpeckers. At Highway 18, follow the byway east, using pull-outs to spot golden eagles, red-shouldered hawks, and sharp-shinned hawks soaring on thermal updrafts. Stop at Heap's Peak Arboretum, where a nature trail provides glimpses of coyotes, gray foxes, dark-eyed juncos, many songbirds, and spring wildflowers. Continue east, through Running Springs, to Big Bear Lake, watching near the road for gray squirrels, coyotes, and deer. Follow Highway 38 to the lake's north side visitor center. The lake hosts abundant wintering waterfowl, including grebes, great blue herons, and white pelicans. Winter bald eagle tours and spring plant walks are a "must." Sparrows are plentiful. Watch for feral burros on the ascent to Onyx Summit; heavy conifers hide northern flickers, white-headed woodpeckers, Townsend's solitaires, and other forest birds. Descend the mountain through the Santa Ana River watershed, watching for deer and black bears. Finish up at Thurman Flats, southern California's largest alder grove and a birding hotspot. Enjoy scores of riparian species, from western toads and Pacific tree frogs to American dippers, orioles, and goldfinches. Continue west to the junction with Interstate 10.

Viewing Information: Songbirds, birds of prey, deer, small mammals, and predators are seen year-round. Songbirds are abundant from spring through fall. Distant views affected by summer smog. Roads closed when snowing. Allow eight hours for trip. *ROADS WINDING, STEEP. USE PULLOUTS.*

Ownership: USFS (714) 866-3437
Size: Ninety-three miles
Closest Towns: Big Bear Lake, Lake Arrowhead, Running Springs

Owls have specialized feathers that allow them to fly without making a sound. They are exceptional hunters, even in total darkness, using their concave facial feathers to pick up and locate the sounds of prey.

Description: The Pacific Crest Trail crosses the slopes above this popular lake, a traditional winter destination for Canada geese, common mergansers, and other waterfowl. Osprey and bald eagles also winter here and are visible on guided boat tours. Walk past roosting great blue herons in South Miller Canyon and watch for black bears and bobcats near the East Mojave River's shallow pools and waterfalls. High-elevation ponderosa pines and incense cedars are inhabited by juncos, mountain chickadees, and Steller's jays. Acorn woodpeckers, western bluebirds, and ground squirrels favor the oak woodlands. Areas with chamise and manzanita yield views of quail, California thrashers, coyotes, and golden eagles; western rattlesnakes also like the brush. Evening visitors may see spotted owls, bats, flying squirrels, and elusive ringtails, a nocturnal mammal.

Viewing Information: More than 130 bird species; many mammals. Birds of prey and wading birds are seen year-round. Look for waterfowl in winter, songbirds in early spring. Small mammals are seen from spring through fall. Visitor center. Site is closed during storms. Eagle boat tours by reservation, January to mid-March; see phone number below; fee. Located on Rim of the World Scenic Byway.

Directions: *At Cajon on Interstate 15, take Highway 138 east twelve miles to lake.*

Ownership: DPR (619) 389-2303
Size: 2,400 acres   **Closest Town:** Hesperia

The gray plumage of this young American white pelican is not a reflection. Dusky feathers distinguish the juveniles from the white adults. White pelicans are much larger than brown pelicans and their nine-foot wingspan rivals that of North America's largest land bird, the California condor.

BRUCE FARNSWORTH

Spotted owls are found in dense conifer forests, particularly old growth forests, where they inhabit snags or tree cavities. In southern California, they also reside in steep canyons shaded by madrones. They seem to tolerate humans, allowing cautious observers to approach close enough for good photos. MICHAEL SEWELL

Description: Grasslands, boulder-strewn hills, and snow-capped peaks encircle cattail marshes on the state's first wildlife area to use reclaimed water. Ponds here are a winter stopover for bald eagles, ring-necked ducks, white-faced ibis, Baird's sandpipers, and other birds. Desert cottontails, southern mule deer, and lesser nighthawks can be spotted near the water. Scores of songbirds migrate through, including tricolored blackbirds, mountain bluebirds, and three species of longspurs. Burrowing owls, peregrine falcons, and other wintering birds of prey hunt by day; the night hunt belongs to six species of resident owls. Burrows in the grasslands are home to endangered Stephen's kangaroo rats. Endangered coastal sage scrub on the Bernasconi Hills shelters greater roadrunners, orange-throated whiptails, and granite spiny lizards.

Viewing Information: More than 240 bird species; second largest inland Christmas bird count in nation. Thirty-nine mammal and thirty-eight reptile and amphibian species. Raptor viewing is good in fall and spring, excellent in winter. High probability of seeing waterfowl and shorebirds in winter, songbirds in winter and spring. Look for mammals and reptiles year-round. Excellent car viewing; short hikes to wildlife.

Directions: From Interstate 215, take Ramona Expressway exit east to Lakeview. Turn north on Davis Road and drive 2.3 miles to DFG headquarters. From Moreno Valley on Highway 60, go south on Theodore Street until pavement begins to turn; go straight here on dirt road (Davis Road) for 3.5 miles.

Ownership: DFG (714) 654-0580
Size: 4,850 acres   **Closest Town:** Moreno Valley

Green-winged teal winter at many California lakes and wetlands, with some breeding in the northeastern part of the state. ART WOLFE

126 BOLSA CHICA ECOLOGICAL RESERVE

Description: This *bolsa chica*, or "little pocket" of restored urban salt marsh is a haven for waterbirds, such as American wigeons, blue-winged teal, lesser scaups, brown pelicans, and great blue herons. Red-necked phalaropes, dowitchers, and other shorebirds feed on mudflats fringed with pickleweed that shelters marsh wrens and endangered Belding's savannah sparrows. From the boardwalk, use binoculars to watch two nesting islands for black skimmers and five tern species, including endangered least terns. Look below the boardwalk for giant sea hares. Utility poles become perches for birds of prey, including ospreys and peregrine falcons. Broad mesas shelter finches, bushtits, and towhees; the grasslands attract burrowing and short-eared owls. Look for wintering monarch butterflies at the bluff overlook eucalyptus grove.

Viewing Information: More than 200 bird species. High probability of seeing shorebirds in fall, waterfowl in winter. Marine birds are seen from April to August, songbirds in spring and summer. Belding's savannah sparrows are easiest to find when singing, in March and April. Look for peregrine falcons in fall, short-eared owls from October through January. *MANY CLOSED AREAS. TERNS NEST IN SAND; DO NOT DISTURB NESTING SITES.*

Directions: *From Highway 405, take Warner Avenue west about three miles to Highway 1 junction and turn south. Continue about one mile on Highway 1 to entrance.*

Ownership: State Lands/leased to DFG (213) 590-5132
Size: 530 acres   **Closest Town:** Huntington Beach

A buzzing trill and chirps originate from pickleweed may be the only hints of the presence of the well-camouflaged Belding's savannah sparrow. These south coast residents, which rely entirely on pickleweed for food, cover and nesting, are endangered because of the loss of southern wetlands.

B. "MOOSE" PETERSON

Description: This shallow estuary bordered by bluffs and homes was saved from development by several local interest groups. Bike, hike, or drive on Back Bay Drive past mudflats concealing littleneck clams, polychaete worms, and marine life eaten by plovers, sandpipers, and other shorebirds. Shallow bay waters shelter anchovies, California killifish, and halibut, which in turn attract buffleheads, mergansers, black skimmers, ospreys, egrets, brown pelicans, and occasional raccoons. Bay nesting islands shelter American avocets, black-necked stilts, and least terns. Endangered light-footed clapper rails and threatened black rails hide in the cordgrass. Pickleweed camouflages endangered Belding's savannah sparrows. Watch for Anna's hummingbirds, yellow-breasted chats, California gnatcatchers, and many hawks and owls.

Viewing Information: Nearly 200 bird species; many mammals. Up to 30,000 birds present from August to April. High probability of seeing wading birds, shorebirds, and waterfowl from October through March. Look for terns from mid-April to mid-July, songbirds in spring and summer. Birds of prey and clapper rails are seen year-round. Listen for rails' clapping calls. Canoe, kayak viewing. Some horse and bike trails at county park.

Directions: *From Highway 405, take the Jamboree Road exit to Back Bay Drive. Turn right and drive .25 mile to reserve.*

Ownership: DFG, (714) 640-6746; Orange County, (714) 640-1751; Bird Hotline, (714) 651-9474

Size: 892 acres   **Closest Town:** Newport Beach

The black-necked stilt sometimes wades belly-deep into water, delicately picking insects from the water's surface. These graceful and conspicuous shorebirds are very common at freshwater and brackish wetlands. The birds are very protective of their nests, sometimes feigning a broken wing or leg to distract predators.

MIKE DANZENBAKER

128 CRYSTAL COVE STATE PARK

Description: Three miles of bluff-backed beaches and rocky points give way to Moro Canyon's riparian woodland, a home to bobcats, coyotes, and many songbirds. Birds of prey hunt the uplands, while gulls, terns, and shorebirds inhabit sheltered beaches. View coastal tidepools and ospreys, brown pelicans, harbor seals, California sea lions, Pacific white-sided dolphins, and endangered gray whales.

Viewing Information: More than 150 bird species. High probability of seeing shorebirds and marine birds in fall and winter, songbirds in spring and summer. Birds of prey and marine mammals can be seen year-round. Watch for whales from December to February. Twenty miles of hiking, bicycling, and equestrian trails. Hike-in, dry camping.

Directions: From Newport Beach, take Highway 1 south 1.8 miles to Reef Point parking lot. Or continue .25 mile to next parking area, for El Moro Canyon.

Ownership: DPR (714) 494-3539
Size: 2,800 acres **Closest Town:** Laguna Beach

129 PALOMAR MOUNTAIN STATE PARK

Description: Beneath the world-famous Palomar Mountain Observatory lies a mile-high wilderness that includes the Doane Valley Natural Preserve. Meadow trails reveal mule deer, coyotes, and red-shouldered hawks. Tree squirrels, Steller's jays, scrub jays, and acorn woodpeckers share this steep-sided valley with migratory nuthatches, warblers, and swallows. Bats, gray foxes, bobcats, and mountain lions may appear at dusk.

Viewing Information: High probability of seeing songbirds in spring and summer. Birds of prey and all mammals are seen year-round. Many trails, roads; views of ocean and desert. California's southernmost population of banana slugs. Visitor center. Handicap-accessible campgrounds. *COUNTY ROAD 56 IS STEEP AND WINDING. RVs AND LARGE CAMPERS SHOULD CONSULT MAP AND USE COUNTY ROAD 7.*

Directions: Take Interstate 15 fourteen miles north of Escondido. Take Highway 76 east 21.3 miles to County Road 56. Turn north, drive seven miles to mountaintop intersection. Turn left, then left again onto State Park Road.

Ownership: DPR (619) 765-0755, (619) 742-3462
Size: 1,800 acres **Closest Town:** Escondido

Description: Sycamores and willows line two creeks as they wind through a pristine foothill canyon featuring one of southern California's finest oak woodlands. Steep slopes covered with endangered coastal sage scrub shelter nesting California gnatcatchers, red-shouldered hawks, and western rattlesnakes. The Green Valley Truck trail weaves among three types of oaks, whose acorns are favored by acorn woodpeckers and mule deer. Identify the rare Engelmann oaks by their white, deeply-grooved bark. The two year-round creeks attract wildlife between March and October, when other streams are dry. Stream banks reveal the tracks of raccoons, gray foxes, and bobcats; dense riparian growth attracts California towhees, lesser goldfinches, Costa's hummingbirds, and other songbirds. Red-tail hawks and turkey vultures circle above dramatic rock outcroppings. The trail climbs to Ramona Dam, a beautiful but strenuous hike.

Viewing Information: Moderate probability of seeing predators, deer, birds of prey, songbirds, and gnatcatchers year-round. Songbirds are seen spring and summer. A pristine, undeveloped site. *NO VEHICLES ON TRUCK TRAIL.*

Directions: *From Interstate 15, take Rancho Bernardo Road exit and turn east. After 1.3 miles, road name changes to Espola Road. Continue 1.9 miles to Green Valley Truck Trail Road and park on left.*

Ownership: DFG (619) 486-7238
Size: 410 acres   **Closest Town:** Poway

Blue Sky's lush, wooded riparian areas provide prey, cover, and denning areas for the gray fox, a dainty canid common in the state. Primarily a night hunter, gray foxes can be spotted during the day in brushy, wooded areas. They are good climbers and may take refuge in trees. MICHAEL SEWELL

131 TORREY PINES STATE RESERVE/ LOS PEÑAQUITOS MARSH

Description: Rugged sandstone cliffs topped by the rare Torrey Pine are laced by trails that overlook one of the few remaining salt marshes in southern California. Trails meander among wind-tortured pines intermixed with ferns and cactus, a place to watch for brush rabbits, bobcats, scrub jays, and California quail. Hillside chaparral shelters California thrashers and loggerhead shrikes; great horned owls and American kestrels hunt near the bluffs. Southern mule deer feed at the marsh, where pickleweed hides endangered Belding's savannah sparrows and light-footed clapper rails. Least terns, green-backed herons, snowy egrets, and other waders feed in the lagoon, an important nursery for many fish. Summer's elegant and Forster's terns are replaced by wintering black brants, surf scoters, killdeer, and plovers. Offshore, watch for bottlenosed dolphins, occasional California sea lions, and gray whales.

Viewing Information: Moderate probability of seeing all birds, deer, and dolphins year-round. High probability of seeing shorebirds and waterfowl in winter, and songbirds in spring. Marine birds are seen in summer, whales in January and February. Good place for dolphins. Visitor center.

Directions: *From San Diego, drive north on Interstate 5 to Carmel Valley Road exit and turn west. For lagoon, drive one mile to McGonigle Road and turn left into North Torrey Pines State Beach entrance. Or to see Torrey pines, continue west on Carmel Valley Road to Camino Del Mar and turn left. Drive about one mile along beach, then turn right uphill to Torrey Pines Reserve.*

Ownership: DPR (619) 755-2063, (619) 452-8732
Size: 2,000 acres   **Closest Town:** San Diego

The common dolphin is a frequent visitor to south coast offshore waters, following fishing boats, traveling in large groups, and dazzling observers with its playful leaps. This vividly-colored dolphin bears an unmistakable hourglass pattern on each flank.

FRANK S. BALTHIS

Description: Endangered coastal sage scrub covers bluffs above the coast's rocky shoreline, a windswept place that offers some of southern California's best views of endangered gray whales. Rock-bound tidepools teem with sea hares, starfishes, sand castle worms, and other marine life. Wandering tattlers, marbled godwits, ruddy turnstones and other shorebird species follow the tides, each using a specialized bill to probe beneath the sand. The Bayside Trail meanders along bluffs patrolled by prairie falcons, great horned owls, and other birds of prey. The offshore skies and water are the domain of cormorants, terns, gulls, and brown pelicans. Wooded thickets near the visitor center hide warblers, towhees, hummingbirds, and many accidentals. Watch here for gray foxes in the mornings and evenings.

Viewing Information: More than 375 bird species. High probability of seeing shorebirds and wading birds in fall and winter, birds of prey and songbirds from fall through spring. Tidepools are best at low tide from October through April. Watch for gray whales from December through February. *PLEASE DO NOT DISTURB OR COLLECT FROM TIDEPOOLS.*

Directions: *In San Diego, from Interstate 5 or 8, take Highway 209 exit south about six miles to entrance.*

Ownership: NPS (619) 557-5450
Size: 145 acres **Closest Town:** San Diego

The endangered gray whale's ten thousand mile migration from the Bering Sea and Arctic Ocean to Mexico is a spectacular annual wildlife-watching event. During the southbound migration in December and January, spouting whales travel close to the coast, sometimes in groups of several dozen. JEFF FOOTT

133 TIJUANA SLOUGH NATIONAL ESTUARINE RESEARCH RESERVE

Description: Southern California's largest estuarine wetland encompasses a federal refuge and state park, and is one of nineteen national estuarine research reserves. The Tijuana River Valley's tidal sloughs, beaches, uplands, and riparian corridors play host to nearly 400 bird species, including six endangered birds. Belding's savannah sparrows, least terns, light-footed clapper rails, and least Bell's vireos nest here. Peregrine falcons winter at the refuge, and brown pelicans are summer visitors. Tidal flats sustain willets, dowitchers, marbled godwits, and sandpipers; snowy plovers nest near dunes inhabited by uncommon globose dune beetles. Many species of ducks and terns seek estuary waters that are home to little blue herons, reddish egrets, and other wading birds. The uplands offer reliable views of desert cottontails, California ground squirrels, coyotes, songbirds, and raptors.

Viewing Information: Wading birds, birds of prey, shorebirds, and small mammals are seen year-round. High probability of seeing songbirds in spring and fall, terns from May to September. Look for rails in summer, pelicans in summer and fall. Waterfowl are abundant in winter. Visitor center at refuge and state park. Excellent wildlife viewing and interpretation at nearby Sweetwater Marsh NWR.

Directions: *From San Diego, take Interstate 5 south to Coronado Avenue West exit. Drive to Third Avenue and turn left. Continue to Caspian Way and turn left to visitor center. For Borderfield Park: Drive south on Interstate 5 to Dairy Mart Road and turn south. Drive about mile to Monument Road; turn right to park.*

Ownership: USFWS, (619) 575-1290; DPR, (619) 575-3613
Size: 3,556 acres   **Closest Town:** Imperial Beach

These showy elegant terns appear at many southern coastal areas, but nest only on gravel beaches or dikes south of San Diego, such as those at Tijuana Slough. Mixed in among the elegant terns there are apt to be royal terns, endangered California least terns, and even black skimmers.

ART WOLFE

134 CUYAMACA RANCHO STATE PARK

Description: Many habitats here are designated wilderness areas, and home to southern mule deer, raccoons, squirrels, and coyotes. Cuyamaca Lake draws cormorants, canvasbacks, and endangered brown pelicans. Abundant birds of prey include red-shouldered hawks, golden eagles in the summer, and wintering bald eagles. Some of the state's largest canyon live oaks shelter acorn and white-headed woodpeckers; four types of pines are populated by Steller's jays, white-breasted nuthatches, and many migratory songbirds. Nights here belong to bats, badgers, bobcats, and mountain lions.

Viewing Information: More than 300 bird species. Birds of prey, songbirds, and mammals can be seen year-round. Songbirds are abundant in spring. Look for waterfowl in fall. For patient observers, lots of mammals. Visitor center. Equestrian trails. *USE CAUTION ON WINDING ROAD.*

Directions: *From San Diego, take Highway 8 east forty miles to Highway 79/ Japatul Road exit and turn north. Follow Highway 79 four miles to entrance.*

Ownership: DPR (619) 765-0755
Size: 25,000 acres   **Closest Town:** Lake Cuyamaca

135 LAGUNA MOUNTAIN RECREATION AREA

Description: This steep-sided, high-elevation plateau includes a 900-acre wet meadow with two seasonal lakes that attract migratory shorebirds and waterfowl. Fall grasses conceal mule deer. Ash-throated flycatchers, solitary vireos, and Bewick's wrens perch in pines near the meadow edge, an area favored by bobcats and ringtails. The oak woodlands shelter mountain quail, black-chinned hummingbirds, and western bluebirds. Tree cavities hide flammulated owls and several woodpecker species. Secluded stream vegetation sustains endangered least Bell's vireos. Many birds of prey. Summer visitors should see western fence lizards, side-blotched lizards, and gopher snakes.

Viewing Information: Songbirds and birds of prey are seen year-round; best viewing in spring. Look for waterfowl and shorebirds in winter, if lakes have water. *SENSITIVE PLANTS; STAY ON MEADOW TRAILS.*

Directions: *From San Diego, take Highway 8 east about forty miles to Sunrise Highway exit. Turn north and drive ten miles to the Laguna Mountain Visitor Information Center.*

Ownership: USFS (619) 445-6235
Size: 2,080 acres   **Closest Town:** Pine Valley

SOUTHERN DESERT

When Water Is Scarce

Desert mountains overlook a remote world where plants and wildlife have adapted to a hot, arid environment. Cactus store rainfall beneath tough skin protected by thorns. Creosote bush roots reach deeply for water. A single leaf can shade insects or small birds. Snakes and lizards find shade beneath plants or among rocks. Most mammals are active at night; kit foxes and kangaroo rats stay cool in underground burrows.

Bighorn sheep can go for several days without drinking. Desert tortoises and kangaroo rats do not drink at all, subsisting on the moisture from plants or seeds. Wildlife species rely on spring-fed oases, rock-basins filled with rainwater, and artifical water sources, called guzzlers, for survival.

Upper Left: Costa's hummingbird
Lower Left: kangaroo rat
Right: bighorn sheep
Illustration: Del Rio-Price and Charly Price

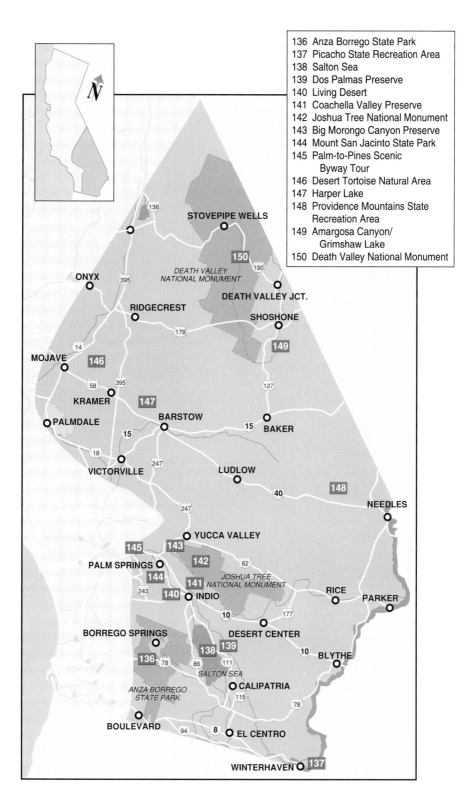

136 Anza Borrego State Park
137 Picacho State Recreation Area
138 Salton Sea
139 Dos Palmas Preserve
140 Living Desert
141 Coachella Valley Preserve
142 Joshua Tree National Monument
143 Big Morongo Canyon Preserve
144 Mount San Jacinto State Park
145 Palm-to-Pines Scenic
    Byway Tour
146 Desert Tortoise Natural Area
147 Harper Lake
148 Providence Mountains State
    Recreation Area
149 Amargosa Canyon/
    Grimshaw Lake
150 Death Valley National Monument

STOVEPIPE WELLS

150

DEATH VALLEY
NATIONAL MONUMENT

190

ONYX

395

DEATH VALLEY JCT.

RIDGECREST

SHOSHONE

178

149

14

MOJAVE

146

127

58   395

KRAMER

147

PALMDALE

BARSTOW

15   BAKER

15

18

247

VICTORVILLE

LUDLOW

40

148

247

NEEDLES

YUCCA VALLEY

145   143

PALM SPRINGS

142

62

144

JOSHUA TREE
NATIONAL MONUMENT

243   140

141

RICE

INDIO

PARKER

10   177

BORREGO SPRINGS

DESERT CENTER

138   139

10   BLYTHE

136   78

86   111

SALTON SEA

ANZA BORREGO
STATE PARK

CALIPATRIA

115

78

BOULEVARD

94   8   EL CENTRO

WINTERHAVEN   137

136 ANZA BORREGO STATE PARK

Description: From sprawling washes and badlands to eroded, mile-high peaks with palm-lined canyons, California's largest state park features desert habitats and wildlife. An underground visitor center is the portal to this vast area traversed by three paved roads and hundreds of miles of backcountry routes and trails. The Borrego Palm Canyon Trail passes a pond with endangered desert pupfish and enters a palm-lined gorge, where migrant warblers and orioles, resident hummingbirds, wrens, phainopeplas, and California quail may be seen. Chuckwallas, desert iguanas, and other reptiles bask on rocks glazed by a patina of "desert varnish." Rare Peninsular bighorn sheep balance on cliff ledges. In the spring, use binoculars to scan the slopes above Tamarisk Grove Campground for *borregos*, or bighorn lambs. Creosote and mesquite shelter Gambel's quail, LeConte's and sage thrashers, long-eared owls, and songbirds. Desert sands bear the tracks of nocturnal Merriam's kangaroo rats, kit foxes, coyotes, bobcats, and mountain lions.

Viewing Information: More than 225 bird species; sixty mammals; sixty reptiles and amphibians. Upland birds and perching birds are seen year-round, songbirds in fall and spring. Moderate probability of seeing thrashers and owls in winter and spring. Wildflowers bloom from March to April. Look for mammals from March to October. Bighorn sheep rut lasts from September through November; lambing occurs January through April. Watch for rams along Road S-22 between markers 12.5 and 13.5. Pull off road completely. Best sheep viewing in morning. *DO NOT APPROACH OR DISTURB BIGHORN SHEEP. SEVERE SUMMER HEAT AND ABRUPT WINTER STORMS. COME PREPARED FOR DESERT CONDITIONS.*

Directions: *From San Diego, take Interstate 8 east forty miles to Highway 79 (Japutal Road). Take Highway 79 north twenty-four miles to Highway 78 and turn east. Drive nineteen miles to Yaqui Pass Road, turn north, and follow signs to visitor center at Borrego Springs. Or from Indio on Interstate 10, take Highway 86 south twenty-five miles to Borrego-Salton Seaway. Turn east and drive twenty-nine miles to visitor center.*

Ownership: DPR (619) 767-5311
Size: 600,000 acres   **Closest Town:** Borrego Springs

The best desert wildlife viewing usually occurs at dawn and dusk, near water. Hide downwind from water source so animals won't see or smell you; use binoculars to get a better view.

Anza Borrego is a landscape of broad slopes and alluvial fans bounded by rugged mountains and sprawling horizons. Its harsh contours are softened by spring blooms of the beavertail cactus and the promise of water at a California fan palm oasis.
LARRY ULRICH

137 PICACHO STATE RECREATION AREA

Description: Take a boat on twelve miles of the Lower Colorado River for close-up views of migratory cormorants, mergansers, white pelicans, and wintering bald eagles. Frogs and soft-shelled turtles inhabit cane- and tule-lined lakes that shelter white-faced ibises, roseate spoonbills, Crissal thrashers, and endangered Yuma clapper rails. Watch here for muskrats, beavers, and southern mule deer, coyotes, bobcats, and raccoons. The surrounding desert is home to Yuma antelope ground squirrels, leaf-nosed bats, and a dozen lizard and snake species. Look near cactus for Gambel's quail, white-winged doves, phainopeplas, and many songbirds. Trails explore rugged backcountry favored by desert bighorn sheep, feral burros, golden eagles, and nesting prairie falcons.

Viewing Information: More than 200 bird species. Watch for raptors, predators, and bighorn sheep year-round. Good views of wading birds, songbirds, deer, and burros year-round. Look for rails in spring. Waterfowl and marine birds are seen in winter. Small mammals are active from spring through fall, reptiles in summer. Good car viewing. *DIRT ROAD IS WINDING AND STEEP. FLASH FLOODS IN LATE SUMMER. COME PREPARED FOR DESERT.*

Directions: *From Winterhaven on Highway 8, take Winterhaven Drive East to Picacho Road and turn north. Continue twenty-five miles (eighteen on dirt).*

Ownership: DPR (619) 339-1360, (619) 393-3059
Size: 7,000 acres   **Closest Town:** Yuma

Prairie falcons usually nest on a rock crevice or cliff ledge. The tercel (male) brings food to the brood, giving it to the female in a spectacular midair exchange. Wild prairie falcon pairs have been used in recovery programs to incubate eggs and raise the young of the endangered peregrine falcon. TOM & PAT LEESON

Description: In 1905, the Colorado River broke through an irrigation project and, for two years, flooded a dry, saline lake bed, creating an inland sea now thirty-five miles long and fifteen miles wide, 235 feet below sea level. Open water, salt marshes, freshwater ponds, and desert scrub attract nearly 400 bird species, including accidentals such as the flamingo, brown booby, and frigatebird. Resident birds include greater roadrunners, Gambel's quail, Albert's towhees, and endangered Yuma clapper rails, among others. View tens of thousands of migratory birds, including fall views of egrets, plovers, brown pelicans, and white pelicans. Huge masses of Canada geese, northern pintails, and Ross' and snow geese arrive in winter, along with bank swallows, gulls, rough-legged hawks, and peregrine falcons. Spring brings many birds of prey, terns, yellow-headed blackbirds, hooded orioles, and white-faced ibises. Summer populations include yellow-footed gulls, black skimmers, American avocets, wood storks, and fulvous tree ducks.

Viewing Information: Shorebirds are seen year-round, particularly in fall and spring. High probability of seeing wading birds year-round; rails are vocal in spring and summer. Waterfowl, birds of prey, and songbirds are seen from fall through spring, terns in spring and summer. View small mammals, predators, reptiles, and endangered desert pupfish year-round. Visitor centers. Each site offers different facilities; call for details. Excellent car viewing. Excellent birding at Whitewater Delta. Restricted viewing during hunting season. *AREA IS VERY HOT APRIL THROUGH SEPTEMBER. ROADS IMPASSABLE AFTER RAIN.*

Directions: *Salton Sea National Wildlife Refuge: From Highway 86/78, take Forrester (Gentry Road) north to Sinclair and refuge entrance. Imperial Wildlife Area: From Niland on Highway 111, drive five miles north on Highway 111, turn west at wildlife area sign and continue two miles. Salton Sea State Recreation Area: From Interstate 10, take Dillon Road/Coachella exit; drive 1.5 miles to Dillon Road and turn right. Turn left on Grapefruit Boulevard, then turn left on Highway 111 and continue twenty-three miles to entrance.*

Ownership: DFG, (619) 359-0577; DPR, (619) 393-3052;
USFWS, (619) 348-5278
Size: 60,200 acres   **Closest Town:** Niland, North Shore

Wildlife viewing and pets don't mix. Dogs frighten wildlife away and diminish viewing experiences. Leave pets at home or in a well-ventilated vehicle. Most natural areas have designated areas where you and your dog can enjoy a romp without harming the habitat or the wildlife.

139 DOS PALMAS PRESERVE

Description: Shady fan palms, perennial seeps, and streams in the upper reaches of Salt Creek form a lush desert oasis for wildlife. Hooded orioles and wintering warblers find shelter among the palms. Giant cane along Salt Creek hides marsh wrens and Salton Sea song sparrows. Artesian water flows to a restored wetland, filling ponds that are home to endangered desert pupfish. Threatened black rails and endangered Yuma clapper rails hide among pond cattails and bulrush that also shelter least bitterns, snowy egrets, and Say's phoebes. The ponds also attract ospreys, lesser scaup, buffleheads, American avocets, and black-necked stilts. The surrounding desert is the domain of phainopeplas and loggerhead shrikes, northern harriers, and prairie falcons. Watch the ground for flat-tailed horned lizards and search mesquites and palo verdes for Abert's towhees, verdins, and other spring migrants.

Viewing Information: Shorebirds, waterfowl, wading birds, and birds of prey are seen year-round; excellent viewing in winter. Songbirds are abundant in spring and fall. Look for reptiles and fish from spring through fall. No facilities here, though many in development. Walk-in viewing; easy, flat terrain. *SUMMERS ARE HOT.*

Directions: From Indio on Highway 111, drive south on Highway 111 twenty-five miles to Parkside Drive and turn left. Drive one mile and turn right on Desertaire Drive. After paved road ends, drive three miles on dirt road to preserve.

Ownership: BLM, (619) 251-0812; TNC, (619) 343-1234; DFG; DPR
Size: 20,000 acres   **Closest Town:** Indio

TOM MYERS

Artesian water has helped restore a wetland and ponds at Dos Palmos Preserve that sustain scores of desert species, including the endangered desert pupfish. Pupfish are just a few inches long. During spawning, the bright blue males vigorously protect their spawning territory by driving off other males. Pupfish may also be seen at site 140.

Description: This desert botanical garden and wildlife park features the plants of ten North American desert regions, and six miles of trails. Greater roadrunners, Gambel's quail, cactus wrens, threatened desert tortoises, and side-blotched lizards may be seen amidst creosote bushes, cacti, or rock mounds throughout the area. Rare Peninsular bighorn sheep graze on rocky slopes. Palm oasis pools shelter endangered desert pupfish, great blue herons, eared grebes, and occasional migrants. Golden eagles, coyotes, badgers, and several types of snakes appear in natural enclosures. A nocturnal exhibit offers excellent views of seldom-seen species, including California leaf-nosed bats, screech owls, and desert kangaroo rats. Resident hummingbirds and mourning doves are joined by a variety of spring songbirds, drawn by the incredible variety of insects and flowering plants in this desert setting.

Viewing Information: Many captive species and some free-roaming residents; excellent year-round viewing. Songbirds are abundant in spring. Many exotic species, exhibits. Good handicap access. Visitor center. Education programs. A site on the Palm-to-Pines Driving Loop.

Directions: From Interstate 10 west of Palm Springs, drive east on Highway 111. Turn right on Highway 74 and drive two miles to Haystack Road; turn left. Drive 1.5 miles and turn right on Portola Road. Parking area is on left. Or from Interstate 10 east of Palm Springs, take Monterey Avenue (Highway 74) to Haystack Road and follow directions above.

Ownership: Living Desert (619) 346-5694
Size: 1,200 acres **Closest Town:** Palm Desert

The barrel cactus serving as a perch for this white-winged dove is also a primary source of food and water. The doves usually nest among mesquite branches. They often feed in large groups and are known for their distinctive "who-cooks-for-you" call.

THE LIVING DESERT

141 COACHELLA VALLEY PRESERVE

Description: Lush fan palm oases border this unusual blowsand desert, a living landscape of dunes and hummocks sculpted by wind, water, and time. Sandfields here sustain endangered Coachella Valley fringe-toed lizards, which escape the summer heat or predators by "swimming" through the sand. The desert landscape camouflages flat-tailed horned lizards, greater roadrunners, lesser nighthawks, and common poorwills. Look among mesquites for Le Conte's thrashers, Gambel's quail, and for nesting black-tailed gnatcatchers and phainopeplas. Chollas hold the flask-shaped nests of cactus wrens. A mile-long trail winds among fan palms at the Thousand Palms Oasis, passing pools inhabited by endangered desert pupfish. The palms shelter many spring migrants and nesting American kestrels. Watch for squirrel burrows at the base of creosote bushes; also sidewinders, jackrabbits, and bobcats.

Viewing Information: Birds of prey, song birds, upland birds, and mammals are seen year-round. Songbird viewing is excellent in spring and fall. Look for reptiles in summer, fish from spring through fall. Equestrian trails. Visitor center. Outstanding cooperative effort required to acquire preserve lands. *EXCEPTIONALLY HOT IN SUMMER.*

Directions: *From Palm Springs area, take Interstate 10 east ten miles to the Ramon Road exit and drive east to Thousand Palms Canyon Drive. Turn north and drive two miles to entrance.*

Ownership: BLM, (619) 251-0812; TNC, (619) 343-1234; DFG; DPR; USFWS
Size: 13,000 acres   **Closest Town:** Thousand Palms

Unlike his mammalian namesake, the leopard lizard can actually change its spots in accordance with the surroundings. This lizard is in its "dark phase," where its spots are obscure and the color bars are obvious. In its "light phase," the pattern is reversed.

WILLIAM R. RADKE

Description: Rugged 5,500-foot peaks give way to Mojave and Sonoran desert ecosystems, an arid landscape known for its dramatic Joshua trees. The tree's dagger-like leaves and cream-colored blossoms are a magnet for cactus wrens, ladder-backed woodpeckers, and Scott's orioles. Yucca night lizards, ground squirrels, and wood rats are usually nearby. Five California fan palm oases provide water, food, and shade to resident house finches, phainopeplas, mourning doves, and Gambel's quail. Western pipistrelles and other bats pass the day among the fronds; day and night, desert cottontails, coyotes, kit foxes, bobcats, and desert bighorn sheep make secretive trips to the water. The lower desert's creosote bush and cacti shelter black-throated sparrows, desert iguanas, and kangaroo rats; a half-dozen rattlesnake species make this desert their home. Be sure to stop at the Twentynine Palms Visitor Center.

Viewing Information: More than 230 bird species; many mammals, reptiles. High probability of seeing songbirds in spring and fall, reptiles from spring through fall. Birds of prey are seen year-round. Low probability of seeing small mammals, predators, and bighorn sheep, all present year-round. Watch for wildlife near oases and water, during mornings and evenings. Three visitor centers. Horse trails; driving tour. *HOT SUMMERS. WINDING, NARROW ROADS.*

Directions: *Main entrance: From Interstate 10, take Highway 62 to Joshua Tree or Twentynine Palms. In town of Joshua Tree, turn south on Park Boulevard to visitor center; in Twentynine Palms, turn south on Utah Trail to visitor center. Or use south entrance off Interstate 10, twenty-six miles east of Indio.*

Ownership: NPS (619) 367-7511
Size: 560,000 acres   **Closest Town:** Twentynine Palms

Joshua trees, bristling with an armor of daggers, are found at desert elevations between 2,000 and 6,000 feet. No less than twenty-five species of birds rely on their cream-colored flowers or pods for food and the tough fibers from their furrowed trunks for nesting materials.
GEORGE WARD

143 BIG MORONGO CANYON PRESERVE

Description: This narrow canyon oasis in the Little San Bernadino Mountains sustains five plant communities and about 250 bird species. Trails lead past cat's claw and Mojave yucca that conceal Gambel's quail, white-tailed antelope squirrels, and side-blotched lizards. Loggerhead shrikes, northern mocking-birds, and scrub jays perch among California junipers. Seemingly barren, the desert washes hide cactus wrens, phainopeplas, Merriam's kangaroo rats, and a variety of snakes. One of the Mojave desert's largest cottonwood and willow woodlands lines a creek favored by raccoons, ringtails, great horned owls, and many songbirds; in the summer, watch here for rare Peninsular bighorn sheep, at dawn and dusk. Look for nesting Virginia rails, marsh wrens, and common yellowthroats from a marsh boardwalk. Nearby fields attract Say's phoebes, Cassin's kingbirds, and several birds of prey.

Viewing Information: Best viewing is from late March to mid-May. Seventy-two nesting bird species; many accidentals. Songbirds are seen year-round; best viewed in spring. Moderate probability of seeing birds of prey and upland birds year-round. Watch for small mammals and predators year-round, at dawn and dusk. Reptiles are seen from spring through fall. Cottonwood Trail handicap accessible. *CLOSED MONDAY AND TUESDAY. HOT SUMMERS. SOME MUDDY TRAILS.*

Directions: *Northwest of Palm Springs on Interstate 10, take Highway 62 north to Morongo Valley. Turn right on East Drive, continuing three blocks to entrance.*

Ownership: BLM, (619) 251-0812;
San Bernadino County, (619) 363-7190; TNC
Size: 3,940 acres   **Closest Town:** Yucca Valley

The distinctive violet-blue crown and elongated throat feathers distinguish the male Costa's hummingbird. This common desert resident flits from flower to flower, using its needle-like bill to extract nectar. Its remarkable wings may beat in a figure-eight pattern up to eighty times a second while it is hovering.

JACK WILBURN

Description: Over two miles high, these craggy peaks, subalpine forests, and fern-bordered mountain meadows form a designated wilderness accessible only by trails or aerial tram. Enclosed tram cars climb steeply past weathered rock walls, affording good views of soaring red-tailed hawks, Cooper's hawks, and golden eagles. Beechy ground squirrels and raccoons inhabit summit rocks; evening visitors may catch a glimpse of elusive ringtails here. The pine canopy is home to Clark's nutcrackers, ravens, northern flickers, and white-headed woodpeckers. Coyotes, mule deer, bobcats, and mountain lions are also residents; they are joined by many spring migrants, including Steller's jays, western tanagers, western bluebirds, and violet-green swallows.

Viewing Information: Low to moderate probability of seeing small mammals and predators from spring through fall. High probability of seeing songbirds and birds of prey in spring and mid-fall. More than seventy miles of trails. Visitor center. Spectacular views. Sudden weather changes; snow. Wilderness permits required for trailhead access and camping. On Pacific Crest Trail. *PLEASE, NO DOGS ALLOWED ON SITE. DO NOT FEED SQUIRRELS OR RACCOONS.*

Directions: *For tram: From Palm Springs area on Highway 111, take Chino Canyon/Aerial Tramway Road exit and turn west. Drive 3.5 miles to tram parking lot. For wilderness trailhead: Take Highway 243 to Idyllwild. In town, register for permit at ranger station.*

Ownership: DPR, (714) 659-2607; USFS, (714) 659-2117
Size: 30,000 acres   **Closest Town:** Palm Springs

A shy, nocturnal mammal, the ringtail may be spotted with some regularity at night in and near Mt. San Jacinto State Park's summit tram building. Ringtails are about the size of a gray squirrel. The tail, nearly as long as the body, is marked with seven sets of alternating black and white bands.

JACK WILBURN

145 PALM-TO-PINES SCENIC BYWAY TOUR

Description and Directions: From Interstate 10 at Banning, Highway 243 weaves south through the brushy, forested San Jacinto Mountains, with vistas of 11,500-foot Mount San Gorgonio and roadside views of southern mule deer, coyotes, bobcats, even mountain lions. Chaparral and oak woodlands at the Indian Vista Overlook support deer, acorn woodpeckers, towhees, and many lizards, including western skinks, alligator lizards, and coast-horned lizards. Continue to Alandale Fire Station, watching the trees for gray squirrels, band-tailed pigeons, and Steller's and scrub jays. At Mountain Center, continue south on Highway 74 through picturesque Garner Valley and watch for western bluebird nesting boxes placed on roadside trees. Great blue herons and Caspian's terns inhabit Lake Hemet, a winter destination for white pelicans, Canada geese, and other waterfowl. Bald eagles and black-shouldered kites hunt near the lake; nearby meadows hide western meadowlarks and valley quail. Highway 74's Cahuilla Tewanet Overlook is an arid world of cactus and pinyon pines favored by pinyon jays, prairie falcons, golden eagles, and many lizards. During the steep descent to Palm Desert, enjoy the view and watch for rare Peninsular bighorn sheep on the rocky ledges. Finish up at the Living Desert (see site number 140), a botanical garden and wildlife park.

Viewing Information: High probability of seeing waterfowl, wading birds, and songbirds year-round. Birds of prey, deer, small mammals, and predators can be seen year-round; look for deer at each stop. Wildflowers bloom in early spring at low elevation, in summer at higher elevation. Interpretive trails. Allow six to eight hours for tour. Distant views may be affected by summer smog. Roads paved, open except for winter storms. *ROADS ARE WINDING AND STEEP. PLEASE USE PULL-OUTS FOR VIEWING.*

Ownership: USFS, (714) 659-2117;
Lake Hemet Municipal Water District, (714) 658-3241
Size: Ninety-seven-mile tour   **Closest Town:** Idyllwild

Highway 243 weaves through the brushy, forested San Jacinto Mountains, offering breathtaking views at many turns. Here, Tahquitz Peak stands out among the snow-capped mountaintops. This wild backcountry sustains many large mammals, including mountain lion, bobcat, coyote, and mule deer.

ED COOPER

Description: Located at the western edge of the Rand Mountains and the Mojave Desert, this land of creosote bush shrub flats supports large numbers of the threatened desert tortoise, California's state reptile. Tortoises live underground in the summer and winter, but watch for them in the spring from trails that wind among carpets of blazing stars, alkali goldfields, and other wildflowers. A half-dozen lizard species, including leopard lizards and whiptails, may be seen sunning or foraging. Creosote bushes serve as perches for loggerhead shrikes and Le Conte's thrashers; they shelter greater roadrunners and chukars, desert kit foxes, and Mojave ground squirrels. Look in the sand for the s-curves of sidewinders or the tracks of badgers and coyotes.

Viewing Information: Moderate probability of seeing tortoises from mid-March to mid-June, lizards from spring to fall. Look for songbirds and birds of prey in spring. More than 150 spring wildflower species. Visitor center. Spring tours; call for reservations. *DO NOT COLLECT OR RELEASE TORTOISES. VERY HOT IN SUMMER, WITH POOR VIEWING.*

Directions: *From Highway 58 or Highway 14, take California City exit to California City. Drive through town; turn north on Randburg-Mojave Road and continue 5.5 miles to entrance.*

Ownership: Desert Tortoise Preserve Committee, (714) 884-9700; BLM (619) 375-7125; DFG
Size: 25,000 acres   **Closest Town:** California City

The desert tortoise, California's state reptile, is rarely seen during summer and winter, but watch for them emerging in the spring, when wildflowers and other foods are abundant. They are considered threatened because more than half of their native habitat has been lost to urbanization, agriculture, mining, and energy development.

DENNIS FLAHERTY

147 HARPER LAKE

Description: The richly vegetated lakes and marshes of this Mojave Desert oasis are a magnet for resident wildlife and thousands of migratory waterfowl, shorebirds, and wading birds. Flocks of white pelicans, northern pintails, mallards, and several species of teal seek this secluded site. Snowy plovers, least sandpipers, and killdeer join northern and Wilson's phalaropes on or close to the muddy shores. Virginia rails breed among wetland vegetation that hides marsh wrens and yellow-headed blackbirds. More than sixteen species of birds of prey have been counted here in a single day, including long-eared owls, burrowing owls, northern harriers, prairie falcons, and golden eagles. One field has sheltered at least 300 feeding short-eared owls.

Viewing Information: Wading birds and songbirds are seen year-round; songbirds are abundant in spring and fall. High probability of seeing waterfowl, shorebirds, and birds of prey from fall through spring. Look for long-eared owls in woodland thickets; short-eared owls are close to marsh. *HEAVY TRAFFIC ON ROAD. HOT IN SUMMER. NO FACILITIES AT SITE.*

Directions: *From Barstow, take Highway 58 twenty-five miles to Harper Lake Road; turn north and drive five miles to lake.*

Ownership: BLM (619) 256-3591
Size: 480 acres   **Closest Town:** Barstow

Short-eared owls are a common winter migrant in the southern deserts, often roosting on the ground in open fields. Large groups of short-eared owls may hunt together in areas where there are abundant rodents, insects, or other prey.

ART WOLFE

Description: Spectacular eastern Mojave scenery. Sun-scorched washes and mesas rise 7,000 feet from Clipper Valley, meeting weathered crags that offer magnificent East Mojave vistas. An ancient ocean, limestone rock, and time formed the cool Mitchell Caverns, home to California myotis bats and rare pseudo-scorpions. Joshua trees, cactus gardens, and creosote sustain threatened desert tortoises, kangaroo rats, greater roadrunners, and ladder-backed woodpeckers. Thirty-five reptiles and amphibian species reside here, including chuckwallas, and green-collared and banded lizards. Resident bushtits, verdins, and wrens are joined by migratory finches, warblers, and orioles. Antelope ground squirrels, coyotes, and gray foxes move through open country at dawn and dusk. Look for elusive desert bighorn sheep near Crystal Spring and watch the skies for nearly a dozen hawk and owl species.

Viewing Information: 140 bird species. Upland birds and birds of prey are seen year-round. High probability of seeing songbirds in April and May, bats year-round. Watch for small mammals and predators year-round; coyotes are readily seen. Reptiles can be seen from May to October. Few trails, open hiking. Remote. BLM land adjacent. *COME PREPARED FOR THE DESERT.*

Directions: *From Interstate 40 about 100 miles east of Barstow, take Essex Road north sixteen miles to visitor center.*

Ownership: DPR (619) 389-2303
Size: 5,900 acres   **Closest Town:** Goffs

The muscular body and massive horns of this desert bighorn ram are a striking emblem of desert tenacity and survival. Desert bighorn sheep can go for several days without drinking. They find water in natural rock basins, called tinajas, in desert pools at palm oases, or at manmade water holes called guzzlers.

TOM & PAT LEESON

149 AMARGOSA CANYON/GRIMSHAW LAKE

Description: The Amargosa River flows year-round through deeply eroded badland canyons, forming lush pools and wetlands surrounded by willows, cottonwoods, and grape thickets. Ruddy ducks, teal, and great blue herons seek the secluded ponds. Sandpipers scurry along shorelines and the riparian border supports abundant songbirds, including blue grosbeaks, willow fly-catchers, and least Bell's vireos and western yellow-billed cuckoos, both endangered. Look here for northern pygmy owls and scan the rock walls for cliff swallows and swifts. Clear water supports Amargosa pupfish and Nevada speckled dace and attracts coyotes, badgers, and small mammals. Drive or hike one mile to Grimshaw Lake, home to the endangered Amargosa vole and a stopover for white-fronted geese, Canada geese, and many ducks and shorebirds. Watch for prairie falcons, northern harriers, and red-tailed hawks.

Viewing Information: High probability of seeing waterfowl, shorebirds, birds of prey, and songbirds from fall through spring. Waterfowl viewing at lake is excellent in winter only. Watch for predators and small mammals year-round, at dawn and dusk. Fish can be seen year-round. *AREA IS HOT IN SUMMER. NO FACILITIES AT SITE.*

Directions: *East of Baker, from Highway 15 take Highway 127 north forty-eight miles. Take Spanish Trail Highway five miles east to Tecopa. Turn on dirt road in front of Tecopa post office, and drive .5 mile to marked trailhead, veering left at cement foundations. To reach the lake, take Tecopa Hot Springs Road one mile north of town of Tecopa Hot Springs.*

Ownership: State Land Commission; BLM, (619) 256-3591
Size: 9,500 acres   **Closest Town:** Tecopa

Greater white-fronted, Canada, and snow geese are not strangers to the desert. Open water, such as Grimshaw Lake, is a magnet for wintering geese, which stopover briefly to feed and rest. The snow geese are easy to identify by their bold black wingtips.

MICHAEL FRYE

Description: A land of startling extremes, from 11,000-foot snow-capped peaks to a spot 282 feet below sea level, with arid dunes, salt pans, lush oases and marshes in between. Even though there is almost no rain and temperatures reach 127 degrees F., there are more than 1,000 species of flowering plants, including ferns, lilies, and orchids. Close to 400 wildlife species breed here, including 290 bird species, fifty-seven mammals, thirty-six reptiles, three amphibians, and five species of pupfish. From a wooden boardwalk, watch the pupfish spawn furiously in Salt Creek's braided streambed. Look for the showy, blue pupfish at Saratoga Springs, habitat favored by wading birds, shorebirds, and waterfowl. Visit Furnace Creek to spot great-tailed grackles, Wilson's warblers, white-throated swifts, and other migrants. Drive a four-by-four up Wild Rose Canyon, where a pinyon juniper woodland shelters resident chukars, black-throated gray warblers, and others. At dusk, evening, or dawn, desert kit foxes and sidewinders appear in the sand dunes at Stovepipe Wells. Watch for desert bighorn sheep on the Scenic Canyon four-wheel-drive routes. Ravens and roadrunners appear everywhere.

Viewing Information: Fish can be seen in March and April. High probability of seeing waterfowl, shorebirds, and songbirds in spring and fall, reptiles from spring through fall. Desert mammals rarely visible during day; best viewing is at dawn and dusk, near water. Visitor center. Guided tours. *COME PREPARED FOR DESERT. SITE IS EXTREMELY REMOTE AND HOT IN SUMMER.*

Directions: *From Interstate 15, take Highway 127 north to Highway 178. Turn west to park. Or from Highway 395, take Highway 178 or 190 east into park. Or from Highway 95 in Nevada, take Highways 267, 374, or 373 west into park.*

Ownership: NPS (619) 786-2331
Size: 2,067,627 acres   **Closest Town:** Furnace Creek

While other desert creatures remain hidden, this member of the cuckoo family is often out in the midday heat. Greater roadrunners dash from bush to bush, with their necks outstretched and tails parallel to the ground, searching for prey. On cold days, they stand with their backs to the sun, relying on their dark-colored feathers to absorb heat.

JOHN HENDRICKSON

SPECIES/SITE INDEX

The numbers following each species are site numbers, not page numbers. This listing represents *some* of the more popular and unusual species in the state, as well as *some* of the best places to see them. The list includes several threatened (T) or endangered (E) species. Very common species, such as ravens, sparrows, or squirrels, are not included in the list.

About Defenders of Wildlife

For more than four decades, Defenders of Wildlife has been one of America's most effective champions of wildlife. With wildlife populations declining, Defenders is promoting new approaches to wildlife conservation that will help species get ahead of the extinction curve. A nonprofit organization founded in 1947, Defenders has over 80,000 members and supporters. Defenders utilizes public education, litigation, and advocacy of progressive public policies aimed at protecting the diversity of wildlife and preserving the habitat critical to its survival.

If you are interested in becoming a member, annual dues are $20, which includes six issues of the bimonthly magazine, *Defenders*. For further information, write or call:

Defenders of Wildlife
1244 19th St. N.W.
Washington, DC 20036
(202) 659-9510

More Books From Falcon Press

The *California Wildlife Viewing Guide* is part of the Watchable Wildlife Series from Falcon Press. This series has been created through the National Wildlife Viewing Program, a Watchable Wildlife partnership initiative coordinated by Defenders of Wildlife. If you liked this book, look for the companion guides that cover other states you plan to visit.

In addition to the Watchable Wildlife Series, Falcon Press specializes in full-color nature books, calendars, and recreational guidebooks. If you want to know more about hiking, fishing, scenic driving, river floating, or rockhounding in your favorite state, check with your local bookstore or call toll-free 1-800-582-2665. When you call, please ask for a free catalog listing all the books and calendars available from Falcon Press.

Falcon Press Publishing Co., Inc.
P.O. Box 1718
Helena, MT 59624
1-800-582-2665